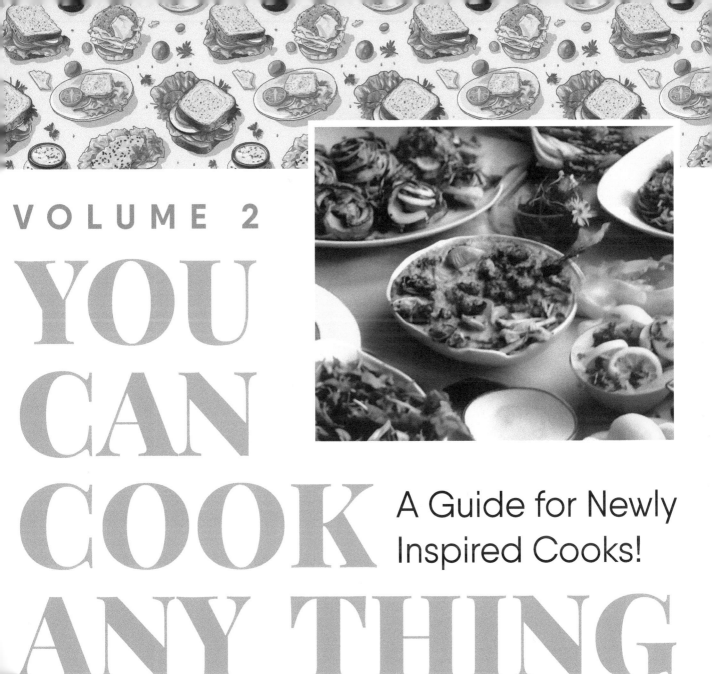

VOLUME 2

YOU CAN COOK ANY THING

A Guide for Newly
Inspired Cooks!

SALAD AND VEGGIE THINGS

JORJ MORGAN
Images by Nick Elia

Video Production by Firetower Media

ISBN: 978-1-963569-50-6 (hard cover)
 978-1-963569-51-3 (soft cover)

Morgan. Jorj.

Published by Warren Publishing
Charlotte, NC
www.warrenpublishing.net
Printed in the United States

For my treasures: Mallory, Ben, Sam, Brooke, and Josh.
Dreams become reality when you work hard and love what you do.
I wish for you to dream BIG! By fulfilling your dreams,
you make dreams come true for others.
You are Nana's dreams come true!

Acknowledgments

First and foremost, thank you to all my food-lovin', recipe-testin', potluck-partyin', bubble-lovin' friends who taste my food and want more. This makes me the happiest cook in the world!

My family: Well you guys are my inspiration for everything. From Joshie's finger food to Brookie's brownies, to Sammy's multi-breakfasts, to Ben's pizza and only pepperoni pizza, to Mallory's love of baking ... you guys are the food that feeds my heart and soul.

To Nick Elia: Man, oh man, are you a talent. Your graphics make me hungry ... Which, of course, is the point. Thank you.

To Joel at Firetower Media: You make me look like Giada. Well, close enough!

To Luca at Creative Enabler: What a technical adventure we've had. I look forward to all the places we will go.

To Amy Crowe: Well, it goes without sayin' ... I couldn't do this without ya!

To Amy and Mindy from Warren Publishing: Thank you for taking a chance on a "wizened" cookbook author for yet another spin on everything yummy.

And to hubby: Well thank you for being my ULTIMATE TASTE TESTER with your no-holds-barred comments and critiques and love of all things food, family, and friends. XOXOXO

Contents

Let's Do This Thing:

Video Demos!

Need a little extra help learning these new cooking techniques? No worries, I've got you! Throughout the book I've included QR codes that link to my demonstration videos so you can see how it's done.

Things to Know

To work your way around all things veggie, you'll need to know a couple terms, learn a bit about vinaigrettes, and bond with a few must-have gadgets.

Let's begin.

Salady Dressing Things

The simplest of all salad dressings is a vinaigrette. Traditionally it is made by combining one part acid with three parts oil. That's the conventional method, but your vinaigrette can be made your way! I like to do a fifty-fifty combination of acid and oil. The acid is usually vinegar but can also be citrus juice or even a brine—like pickle juice! The oil can be olive oil, either virgin or extra virgin, but it can also be a unflavored oil like grapeseed or an emulsified oil like mayonnaise. The secret is to mix the ingredients together well by using a whisk, a blender, a food processor, or by simply shaking everything together in a jar. Once you have mastered vinaigrette, you can add any ingredients you want to add extra oomph to your veggie salad.

Prepping Things

My rule on veggies is to choose the freshest veggie you can find. Spend some time at the farmers market exploring what is seasonably available. It's amazing how much you learn talking to the famers and feeling the passion they bring to all things veggie and fruit.

Whether you buy from the market or the grocery store, when you get the produce home, spend an extra bit of time preparing it to use during the week. Rinse lettuce leaves and spin dry. Place these into resealable plastic bags. Use a fork to pierce the bags to let the air flow around the lettuce.

There you have it: a perfect way to start your nightly salad.

Prepping Veggies

Wash and peel veggies you know you are going to use over the next few days. Veggies will keep fresh in airtight containers for several days in the fridge. Dice onions, carrots, and peppers to use for sauces and sautés. Slice the white (and green) parts of a green onion.

Speaking of peppers, when dealing with hot peppers, you can prepare these in advance too, just remember to wash your hands, especially when handling the seeds and veins.

You can break heads of cauliflower and broccoli into florets and store in resealable bags or containers. You can even blanch or steam veggies like Brussels sprouts or roast veggies like beets and potatoes to get a head start on Citrus Marinated Beets or Pommes de Terre Chantilly. (Is your mouth watering yet?)

Any THING you can do to prep for the busy week ahead will give you extra time to spend with family and friends.

VIDEO: Prepping lettuce

VIDEO: Handling hot, HOT peppers

Things That Chop, Slice, & Dice

Using certain gadgets and appliances will help you turn that everyday veggie into a five-star meal. Here are a few of my favorites.

- **A food processor** with attachments will make short work out of chopping, slicing, and shredding. It is also the perfect gadget to use to make vinaigrettes and salad dressings. There are large and mini versions. Choose the one that best fits into your kitchen space.

- **A blender** can also emulsify salad dressing ingredients.

- **A mandoline slicer** creates very thin slices of your veggie thing. You can also use a handheld slicer for this task. Use both carefully. Watch out for fingertips!

- **A zester** can also be used for the finer tasks. You can use little bits of lemons, limes, or orange peel to produce major blasts of flavor. So do garlic cloves and ginger roots.

A few knifey terms:

- **Chop** means to cut the thing into small pieces. If you are chopping a peeled onion, slice it in half and then in half again. Then chop the wedges into small pieces. Usually, you chop things to use in soups or stews. Chopped things cook down into smaller, bite-size pieces.
- **Dice** means to chop the thing into small, equal-size cubes. Take that same peeled onion (with top and bottom stems in place) and cut off the fuzzy end. Use your knife to cut slices from the top to almost the bottom of the onion. By not cutting all the way through, the onion stays together. Now turn that onion a quarter turn and cut slices down again, creating squares. Rotate the onion ninety degrees and cut down so the squares fall onto your work surface. You diced!
- **Fine dice** just means really, really small squares.
- **Julienne** means to cut the thing into long strips. This time, we're going to use a bell pepper. Cut the pepper in half and remove the inside seeds and veins. Cut the pepper in half again. Lay a quarter piece of pepper, cut side down, on your work surface. Use you knife to cut thin slices from the top to the bottom of the pepper. You can cut the tips of the strips to create equal lengths of pepper.
- **Mince** means really chopping so much, the small pieces stick together and become paste-like. Take a piece of that onion. Use your knife to chop the thing into the tiniest pieces possible. Then take the flat blade of your knife and move it back over the pieces to squish them together, making them into a paste. You can buy a hand tool that minces cloves of garlic and small bits of onion. My favorite tool for mincing is a mini food processor. This is an affordable gadget that chops and minces in minutes.

Boiling, Blanching, Steaming, Roasting, & Grilling

These are the veggie preparations that you use most often.

- **Boiling:** You can cook a veggie by placing it into boiling water. When it is tender, transfer the veggie to an ice water bath to stop the cooking process and to retain its vibrant color.
- **Steaming:** You can steam the veggie by putting it in a basket or colander over boiling water. Transfer to an ice water bath here too.
- **Blanching:** You can partially cook the vegetable using the same methods mentioned above. Simply cook for a shorter amount of time. Now we're blanching!
- **Roasting:** Roast a vegetable in the oven over medium-high heat, 375° to 400°. Place it onto a sheet pan and douse in olive oil and your favorite spices. You can roast more than one vegetable at a time.
- **Grilling:** An outdoor grill or an indoor grill pan will cook veggies with char marks and crisp little bits on the edges. Slice eggplant or zucchini into at least half-inch pieces so that they hold up to the grilling process. Use olive oil to make sure the veggie doesn't stick.
- **Frying:** Oh! And let's not forget frying. Who doesn't like a golden, crisp wedge of potato or a hot, crunchy buttermilk-battered pickle? Thing to remember here is make sure your oil is hot (375°) and stays hot. And don't overfill you pot. When the veggie is placed into the hot oil, the liquid will bubble up, so leave lots of room.

Veggies are the most versatile THING we have in our meal-planning arsenal. Let's take a look at some great recipes for you to use for your future inspirations.

VIDEO: Blanching veggies

VIDEO: Using a grill pan

Salady Things to Know

In this book, I'll give you tools to elevate your lettuce side salad by creating salad bowls that you will fall in love with. You can put any THING into a salad bowl and make it a total meal. The beauty of a fresh salad is all the fruits and veggies you can use as salad ingredients— eat a rainbow! This is also an excellent way to use up leftovers, which allows you more creativity in the kitchen in the first place. Let's start with salad dressings.

Salady Things

BASIC VINAIGRETTE IS A COMBINATION OF FAT AND ACID. The fat is oil. You can use olive oil, which can be light (virgin), heavy (extra virgin), or flavored. This has to do with the pressing of the olives, but for our purposes, it has to do with taste. If you want the dominant flavor of your dressing to be olivey, you go with extra virgin olive oil. If you like a lighter flavor, virgin olive oil is the way to go. You can find specialty olive oils that infuse flavors like lemon or chilis. These are totally worth trying. For even lighter dressings, you can choose vegetable oil. It all works. Dip a piece of bread into the oil before you use it in your dressing to make sure it tastes the way you like it.

Acidity in a dressing can come from citrus, vinegar, or a combination of both. Here you want to choose the flavor that compliments the other components in the dish. There are many flavors of vinegar. You simply have to look on the shelves at your grocery store to see the different varieties. It's kinda like the difference between pickles: some are way more sour tasting than others. Sample vinegars with cucumber or lettuce dippers to find your favorite flavors. Add lemon, lime, or orange juice and fresh herbs to bring your dressing to the next level. There is a vinaigrette tradition about adding three parts oil to one part vinegar, but I vary that all the time. My rule of thumb is the sourer you like your pickles, the more vinegar you use in your vinaigrette.

Let's try it out!

Lemon Balsamic Vinaigrette
makes about 1 cup
10 minutes till it's ready

- ⅓ cup white balsamic vinegar
- juice from 1 lemon, about 3 tablespoons
- ½ cup virgin olive oil
- ½ teaspoon kosher salt
- ½ teaspoon coarse black pepper

1. Pour the vinegar into a small bowl or measuring cup. Whisk in the lemon juice.
2. Slowly pour in the olive oil while you continue to whisk.
3. Season with salt and pepper.
4. The dressing should be well blended with no separation between the oil and the vinegar.

Thing to Note:
Use this basic recipe to create any kind of vinaigrette. Just a teaspoon of Dijon-style mustard whisked into the vinegar and lemon, and a clipping of fresh dill tossed in before serving will create a yummy finish to your salad.

Easy Vinaigrette

VIDEO: Making an easy vinaigrette

Now let's make a simple salad that works well with this vinaigrette.

"My Way" Green Salad
with Olives and Feta Cheese
serves 4
30 minutes till it's ready

- 1 head green leaf lettuce, stem removed, torn into bite-size pieces, 4 to 6 cups
- 1 bunch loosely packed baby spinach leaves, torn into bite-size pieces, about 4 cups
- 2 cups loosely packed arugula leaves, torn into bite-size pieces
- 1 cup sweet baby tomatoes, cut in half
- 1 baby cucumber, sliced in half lengthwise, seeded, and cut into bite-size pieces, about 1 cup
- 2 to 3 very thin slices of red onion, cut into bite-size strips, about ¼ cup
- 2 tablespoons chopped fresh basil
- Lemon Balsamic Vinaigrette

1. Place the lettuce, spinach, and arugula into a bowl. Toss with tomatoes, cucumber, and red onion. Sprinkle basil into the mix.
2. Spoon dressing over the salad. You want to lightly dress the leaves to avoid a soggy salad.
3. Season with salt and pepper.

Thing to Note:
Don't be afraid to substitute any of your favorite lettuces here. You will find that sturdier lettuces like iceberg and romaine can handle more dressing, while lighter leaves, like the ones in this salad, require only a couple of spoonfuls.

One last bit of info for your salad dressings: you don't need to stack bottles of dressings in your fridge. You can use the ingredients that you have on hand to create something delicious. Here are a couple of my favorites.

Homemade Ranch Dressing
makes about 1 cup dressing
10 minutes till it's ready

- ⅔ cup buttermilk
- ½ cup mayonnaise
- 2 teaspoons Worcestershire sauce
- 1 tablespoon chopped fresh chives
- 1 tablespoon chopped fresh dill
- 1 tablespoon chopped fresh parsley
- ½ teaspoon onion powder
- ½ teaspoon garlic powder
- ½ teaspoon kosher salt
- ½ teaspoon coarse black pepper

1. Whisk together the buttermilk, mayonnaise, and Worcestershire sauce.
2. Stir in the fresh herbs.
3. Stir in the onion and garlic powders, and season with salt and pepper.

Thing to Note:
No buttermilk? No problem. Simply add 2 tablespoons of fresh lemon juice or white vinegar to a measuring cup. Pour milk to the ⅔-cup line. Let sit a second or two, and you're good to go.

Chunky Blue Cheese Dressing

makes about 1 cup dressing
10 minutes till it's ready

- ½ cup buttermilk
- ¼ cup whole milk
- ¼ cup sour cream
- 3 ounces blue cheese, crumbled, about ½ cup
- 1 teaspoon white balsamic vinegar
- ½ teaspoon Worcestershire sauce
- ½ teaspoon kosher salt
- ½ teaspoon coarse black pepper

1. Whisk together the buttermilk, whole milk, and sour cream.
2. Stir in the blue cheese crumbles.
3. Stir in the vinegar and Worcestershire sauce and season with salt and pepper.

Asian Sesame Dressing
makes about 1 cup dressing
10 minutes till it's ready

- ¼ cup rice wine vinegar
- 2 tablespoons honey
- 1 (2-inch) piece fresh ginger, peeled and grated, about 2 tablespoons
- 2 tablespoons sesame oil
- ½ cup vegetable oil
- ½ teaspoon garlic powder
- ½ teaspoon kosher salt
- ½ teaspoon coarse black pepper

1. Whisk together the vinegar, honey, and ginger.
2. Whisk in the sesame and vegetable oils.
3. Stir in garlic powder, salt, and pepper.

VIDEO: Peeling and mincing ginger

You Can Cook Any THING

Mince Ginger

Chili-Lime Salad Dressing
makes about 1 cup dressing
10 minutes till it's ready

- zest from 2 limes, about 2 teaspoons
- juice from 2 limes, about 4 tablespoons
- ¼ cup red wine vinegar
- 1 tablespoon soy sauce
- 1 tablespoon honey
- ⅓ cup extra virgin olive oil
- 1 garlic clove, finely minced
- ½ teaspoon red pepper flakes
- 1 teaspoon ground cumin
- 1 teaspoon kosher salt

1. Whisk together the lime zest and juice, vinegar, soy sauce, and honey in a bowl.
2. Slowly incorporate the olive oil.
3. Stir in the garlic, red pepper flakes, cumin, and salt.

There's no salad more well known than Caesar salad. It's a classic dish that stars on menus in fine dining establishments to this day. The original salad dressing is made with a raw egg. I abandoned the egg early on and find my Caesar is just as good without it. And I know what you're thinking—must I use anchovies? But trust me, this salad needs anchovies like a baked potato needs butter. If you really don't like the idea of using anchovy fillets, you can substitute with anchovy paste.

Classic Caesar Salad
serves 4 to 6
20 minutes till it's ready

- 2 medium garlic cloves, minced, about 2 teaspoons
- 1 tablespoon Dijon-style mustard
- 1 tablespoon Worcestershire sauce
- 1 (2-ounce) tin anchovy fillets, packed in oil
- 1 large head romaine lettuce, washed, dried, and torn into strips, about 6 to 8 cups
- juice of 1 medium lemon, about 3 tablespoons
- ¼ cup balsamic vinegar
- 1 cup croutons
- 4 ounces Parmesan cheese, grated, about 1 cup
- 1 teaspoon (or more) coarse black pepper

1. Place the garlic, mustard, Worcestershire sauce, and anchovies (with their oil) into a large, wooden bowl. Use the back of a wooden spoon to smash everything together until it becomes a paste.
2. Add the romaine leaves to the bowl, sprinkle with lemon juice, and drizzle the vinegar over top.
3. Add the croutons and Parmesan cheese. Drizzle with half of the olive oil.
4. Toss everything together, making sure you get all the good stuff from the bottom of the bowl.
5. Taste and add oil as desired. Season with coarse black pepper.

Thing to Note:
If you don't have a wooden bowl for your salad, or if you are making a BIG batch of dressing, you can make the salad dressing in advance by using a blender. Place the garlic, mustard, Worcestershire, anchovies, and balsamic vinegar into a blender. Pulse to combine. With the machine running, gradually add the olive oil. Season with salt and pepper. This dressing will be thick and creamy and will last in a resealable container for a week or more in your fridge.

Once you've mastered the classic Caesar, you can switch things up and make your own version of Caesar salad. Here's one of my favorite variations.

Street Corn Caesar Salad
serves 4
30 minutes till it's ready

For Caesar dressing:
- 5 to 6 garlic cloves
- ½ cup balsamic vinegar
- ¼ cup red wine vinegar
- juice of 1 medium lemon, about 3 tablespoons
- 1 tablespoon Dijon-style mustard
- 1 tablespoon Worcestershire sauce
- 1 (2-ounce) tin anchovy fillets, packed in oil, drained
- ½ cup olive oil
- 1 teaspoon kosher salt
- 1 teaspoon coarse black pepper

1. Place the garlic, vinegars, lemon juice, mustard, Worcestershire sauce, and anchovies into the bowl of a food processor (or blender). Pulse to emulsify.
2. With the machine running, slowly pour in the olive oil. Taste and season with some of the salt and pepper.
3. Pour the dressing into a resealable container. You will have more than you need. The dressing will keep in the fridge for a week (or more).
4. Place the corn onto a grill, over medium-high heat, and cook, turning occasionally, until many of the kernels are golden brown. This will take several minutes. Remove the corn and cool. Cut the kernels from the cobs into a bowl. Add the corn chip crumbs and half of the cheese. Drizzle two tablespoons of the dressing over the corn filling and toss.
5. Cut each head of lettuce in half. Trim the stems and top leaves. Lay the lettuce onto a platter, cut side up. Spoon the corn filling over the lettuce, stuffing it into the leaves. Spoon more Caesar dressing over the salad, just moistening the leaves. Top with the remaining cheese and black pepper.

For corn filling:
- 4 ears corn
- 1 cup corn chips crushed into fine crumbs
- 4 ounces Parmesan cheese, shredded, about 1 cup

For salad:
- 2 medium heads romaine lettuce

Thing to Note:
Smash those chips however you like, but make sure that you have very fine crumbs. I pulse mine in a food processor, but you can place them in a resealable plastic bag and crush them with a rolling pin, fry pan, or meat mallet.

Another Thing to Note:
I used corn chips the first time I made this salad, but any little corny thing will work. Cornbread crumbs, cheese, butter crackers, or even crunched up cheese straws are a great balance to the kernels for this filling.

Chop chop! That's the rule for this next salad. The idea is that all the ingredients are cut to the same bite-size perfection. Then when you add the dressing, it coats each morsel evenly. There are entire restaurants based on the chopped salad. I even found a pair of scissors with multiple blades just for chopping salad ingredients! What will they think of next?

Layered Chopped Salad

serves 4 to 6
30 minutes till it's ready

For dressing:
- 1 cup sour cream
- ¼ cup ketchup
- juice of 1 medium lime, about 2 tablespoons
- 2 tablespoons capers, drained and rinsed
- ½ small white onion, peeled and chopped, about ½ cup
- ½ teaspoon chili powder
- ½ teaspoon ground cumin
- ¼ cup olive oil
- ½ teaspoon kosher salt
- ½ teaspoon coarse black pepper

For salad:
- 1 large head iceberg lettuce, cut into bite-size pieces, about 5 to 6 cups
- 1 cup tortilla chips, crumbled
- 4 ounces cheddar cheese, shredded, about 1 cup
- 1 bunch (6 to 8) green onions, chopped into small pieces, about 1 cup
- 1 pint ripe cherry tomatoes or mixed baby tomatoes, chopped in half, about 2 cups
- 1 large cucumber, seeded and chopped into small cubes, about 1 ½ cups
- 3 carrots, chopped into small cubes, about 1 cup
- 6 whole radishes, stems removed and chopped into small pieces, about 1 cup
- 1 large yellow bell pepper, seeded and chopped, about 1 cup
- 2 tablespoons chopped fresh cilantro

1. Place the sour cream, ketchup, lime juice, capers, onion, chili powder, and cumin into a blender. Pulse to puree.
2. With the machine running, slowly drizzle in the olive oil.
3. Season with salt and pepper.
4. Place the lettuce into a bowl. Drizzle with 2 to 3 tablespoons dressing. Toss until lightly coated.
5. Layer half of the dressed lettuce into the bottom of a large glass bowl. Sprinkle half of the tortilla chips and half of the cheese on top of the lettuce.
6. Next add half of onions, tomatoes, cucumbers, carrots, radishes, and yellow pepper. Drizzle with 2 tablespoons of the dressing.
7. Complete the salad by repeating steps with the remaining ingredients. Drizzle the remaining salad dressing on top of the layered salad. Garnish with chopped fresh cilantro.

VIDEO: Making a layered salad

You Can Cook Any THING
Layered Salads

Watermelon Beet Caprese Salad
with Peach Vinaigrette
serves a crowd
30 minutes, plus an hour or so to roast the beets

For salad:
- 6 medium beets
- 1 small seedless watermelon
- 6 to 8 medium tomatoes, thinly sliced
- 1 pound fresh mozzarella, sliced into thin rounds
- 1 bunch fresh basil leaves
- 1 teaspoon kosher salt
- ½ teaspoon coarse black pepper
- 4 slices bacon, cooked, chopped

1. Preheat your oven to 375°.
2. Wrap the beets in aluminum foil and place them into a baking dish. Roast until the beets just begin to soften, about 1 to 1 ½ hours.
3. Remove the baking dish from the oven and let the beets cool to room temperature. Remove the skin by rubbing with paper towels. Use a mandoline or handheld slicer to slice the beets as thin as possible.
4. Cut the watermelon into ¼-inch slices. Use a round cookie cutter to cut circles in the watermelon slices about the same size as the beets and tomatoes.
5. Assemble the salad by alternating slices of tomato, mozzarella, watermelon, and beet. Continue overlapping slices until the platter is filled. Tuck leaves of basil in gaps and around the edges.
6. Season with salt and pepper.
7. Top with bacon pieces.
8. Chill the salad while you make the vinaigrette.
9. Place the shallot, peach, and basil into a mason jar. Pour in the vinegar and olive oil. Season with salt and pepper. Screw the lid on tightly and shake to combine.
10. When you are ready to serve, use a spoon to drizzle some of the vinaigrette over the salad.

For vinaigrette:
- 1 medium shallot, peeled and finely diced, about ¼ cup
- 1 ripe peach, peeled, pitted, and finely diced, about 1 cup
- 2 tablespoons chopped fresh basil
- ¼ cup vinegar (I use peach-infused white balsamic)
- ½ cup olive oil (I use lime-infused extra virgin olive oil)

Thing to Note:
A mandoline is a tool that you use to get very thin slices from veggies. There are simple handheld mandolines, and there are ornate machines that stand on their own while you press the veggie back and forth over the blade. With either gadget, the thing you must remember is that the blade is sharp. Make sure to use a thick glove when you are slicing. And let that little last bit of veggie go ... you don't need to slice your finger to get one more piece.

VIDEO: Roasting beets

Fresh veggies are no-brainers in your everyday salad bowl. But salads can include cooked veggies and grains too. The more veggies, the better. The seasonings that you flavor your veggies with will lead you to the choice of dressing. For this version, lemon and pine nuts go great together.

Roasted Veggie Salad
with Quinoa
serves a crowd
60 minutes till it's time to eat

- 1 medium butternut squash, peeled, seeded, and cut into 1-inch cubes, about 3 to 4 cups
- 6 to 8 carrots, peeled and cut into 1-inch pieces, about 2 to 3 cups
- 6 to 8 parsnips, peeled and cut into 1-inch pieces, about 2 ½ to 3 cups
- 2 red onions, peeled and cut into wedges, about 2 cups
- 10 to 12 baby portobello mushrooms, stemmed
- 1 teaspoon kosher salt
- 1 teaspoon coarse black pepper
- ½ cup butter, melted, 1 stick
- juice of 1 lemon, about 3 tablespoons
- 1 cup uncooked quinoa
- 1 bunch fresh basil, chopped
- 4 ounces Parmesan cheese, shaved, about 1 cup
- ¼ cup pine nuts, toasted

1. Preheat your oven to 425°.
2. Place the butternut squash, carrots, parsnips, onion wedges, and mushrooms onto a baking sheet.
3. Season with salt and pepper.
4. Stir the melted butter and lemon juice together in a bowl. Pour half of this onto the vegetables. Toss to coat.
5. Roast the veggies until they begin to turn golden brown, about 20 to 30 minutes. Remove the pan from the oven. Place the veggies into a large bowl.
6. Cook the quinoa according to the directions on the package.
7. Season with salt and pepper.
8. Add the quinoa into the bowl. Toss in the basil, Parmesan cheese, and pine nuts.
9. Pour in remaining lemon-butter sauce.
10. Toss and serve warm or at room temperature.

Thing to Note:
This is a yummy main course salad on a day when you're craving a meat-free meal. You can absolutely change out the veggies for anything you have in your fridge and substitute with your favorite herbs and nuts. You can even change out quinoa for orzo pasta. It all works!

VIDEO: Cutting and roasting a butternut squash

Mayo Salady Things

IF YOU HAVE A SCOOP OF MAYO AND LEFTOVER CHICKEN, YOU HAVE EVERYTHING YOU NEED FOR CHICKEN SALAD. The same is true for leftover ham, hard-boiled eggs, salmon, and cooked shrimp. Combine any of these with mayo and—YUM!—you have ham salad, egg salad, salmon salad, and shrimp salad. The possibilities are endless.

Next, there are the things we can add into those salads. Bits of crunchy veg like onion, bell pepper, and celery give your mayo salad a crunch. Canned things like capers, roasted peppers, and water chestnuts are good too. So are pickly things like sweet pickle relish, chopped dill pickles, or even more sour cornichons. Things like fresh herbs and dried spices flavor your mayo sandwiches as do citrusy things like lemons, limes, and oranges. There are so many things that can go into your mayo salad, and you can create your own in just a few minutes using things you have on hand. Here's a couple of guideline recipes to get you started.

"My Way" Egg Salad
serves 2
30 minutes till it's ready

- 4 large eggs (older eggs are better than fresher ones here)
- 4 to 6 cornichons, finely diced, about 2 tablespoons
- 2 to 3 green onions, finely diced, about 2 tablespoons
- ½ celery rib, finely diced, about 2 tablespoons
- 2 tablespoons chopped fresh dill
- ¼ cup mayonnaise
- 1 teaspoon kosher salt
- ½ teaspoon coarse black pepper

1. Place the eggs into a pot with a lid and cover the eggs with water. Cover the pot and bring to a boil over medium-high heat.
2. Once the water is boiling, turn off the heat.
3. Keep the lid on the pot let sit for 11 minutes.
4. Remove the lid and transfer the eggs to a bowl filled with ice water. Cool the eggs to room temperature.
5. Peel the eggs. Chop them into very small pieces and place into a bowl.
6. Add the cornichons, onions, celery, and dill.
7. Fold in the mayonnaise.
8. Season with salt and pepper and stir one more time.

Thing to Note:
Now that you have egg salad, here are some ways to make the most of the most:
- Spoon egg salad into a tomato that is sliced to open like a flower.
- Layer egg salad onto a flour tortilla, adding arugula leaves and thin slices of pickled red onion. Wrap it up for an egg salad wrap like none other.
- Here's my favorite: Slather some mayo onto a piece of rye bread. Spoon egg salad on top of the mayo and add a thick slice of Swiss cheese. Add a thin slice of tomato and slather a bit more mayo on a second slice of bread. Place that on top of the cheese (mayo side down of course) using your hands to mush the sandwich together. Yum oh yummm!

VIDEO: All about eggs

Thyme-Roasted Chicken Salad
with Apples and Almonds
serves 4
30 minutes till it's ready

For chicken:
- 2 large (6- to 8-ounce) skinless, boneless chicken breast halves
- 1 teaspoon kosher salt
- ½ teaspoon coarse black pepper
- 1 tablespoon olive oil
- fresh thyme sprigs

For salad:
- 2 medium apples, peeled and cut into ½-inch dice, about 2 cups
- 2 to 3 celery ribs, thinly sliced, about 1 cup
- 1 (4-ounce) can sliced water chestnuts, drained
- 1 cup sour cream
- ½ cup mayonnaise
- juice of 1 medium lemon, about 3 tablespoons
- 1 teaspoon ground cinnamon
- 1 teaspoon curry powder
- 1 cup sliced almonds
- 2 tablespoons chopped fresh thyme
- lettuce
- tomato wedges
- cucumber slices

Thing to Note:
You can shortcut this mayo salad by using leftover roasted chicken. You can also add things to feed more people. Try adding 2 cups of cooked wild rice or 1 cup of cooked pasta, like fusilli or rotini. Diced pineapple, halved grapes, and thinly sliced radishes also add a tasty kick.

1. Preheat your oven to 350°.
2. Place the chicken breasts into a baking dish. Season with salt and pepper. Drizzle with olive oil. Place thyme springs in and around the chicken.
3. Roast until the chicken is cooked through (reaching an internal temperature of 165°), about 20 to 30 minutes.
4. Cool to room temperature and cut into ½-inch cubes.
5. Place the chicken, apples, celery, and water chestnuts into a bowl.
6. Whisk together the sour cream, mayonnaise, and lemon juice in another bowl.
7. Stir in the cinnamon and curry.
8. Season with salt and pepper.
9. Pour the dressing into the chicken, apple, and celery mixture. Toss to coat.
10. Fold in the sliced almonds and chopped fresh thyme.
11. Season with salt and pepper.
12. Serve the salad on a bed of lettuce and garnish with tomato wedges and cucumber slices.
13. Taste and season with salt and pepper if needed.

VIDEO: Roasting chicken

Ham Salad Spread Three Ways

serves 6 for an appy
30 minutes till it's ready

- 8 ounces cooked ham (ham steak or deli ham), chopped
- 2 to 3 celery ribs, chopped, about 1 cup, plus more for serving
- 2 to 3 green onions, chopped, about ¼ cup
- 2 tablespoons sweet pickle relish
- 1 cup mayonnaise
- 1 tablespoon yellow mustard
- ½ teaspoon kosher salt
- ½ teaspoon coarse black pepper
- 1 English cucumber (seedless cucumber), cut into 2-inch rounds

1. Place the ham, celery, and onions into the bowl of a food processor. Pulse to combine into very small pieces about the size of crumbs, about 5 pulses.
2. Add the relish, mayo, and mustard. Pulse to combine.
3. Season with salt and pepper and pulse one last time.
4. Spread the ham salad onto celery ribs. Scoop the centers from the cucumber rounds (leaving a border on the bottom to hold the salad). Fill the cucumber rounds with ham salad. Serve the remaining ham salad in a bowl to spread on crackers.

Shrimp Salad
in Avocado Bowls
serves 4
20 minutes till it's ready

- 1 pound frozen, cooked medium shrimp (41 to 50 per pound); thawed, peeled, and tails removed
- ¼ cup mayonnaise
- ¼ cup sour cream
- 1 stalk celery, finely diced, about ½ cup
- 1 small shallot, finely diced, about 2 tablespoons
- juice of ½ fresh lemon, about 2 tablespoons
- 1 tablespoon chopped fresh dill
- 1 tablespoon chopped fresh parsley
- 1 teaspoon kosher salt
- ½ teaspoon coarse black pepper
- 2 ripe avocados

1. Place the thawed, cooked shrimp into a bowl.
2. In a separate bowl, whisk together the mayo and sour cream. Stir in the celery, shallot, lemon juice, dill, and parsley. Season with salt and pepper.
3. Pour the dressing over the shrimp and toss to coat.
4. Cut the avocados in half and remove the pits. Drizzle the cut side of the avocado with more lemon juice, salt, and pepper.
5. Scoop the shrimp salad into the holes left by the pits in the avocado.
6. Garnish with more fresh herbs.

Thing to Note:
I use small shrimp in my shrimp salad, but you can choose whichever size you like, or you can also choose to chop the shrimp into small pieces. Every THING works!

Now that we've explored fresh salads of all types, let's talk about some of the other veggies that are hanging around!

Veggie Things

EAT A RAINBOW—THAT'S THE SAYING TO LIVE BY! Veggies are, of course, good for you.

Every culture uses vegetables in their dishes. There's Italian flavored eggplant, Asian spiced

broccoli, Mexican smashed avocados for guacamole, and French-inspired asparagus

poached in fresh cream. Although fresh vegetables are wonderful, I never turn up my nose at

frozen ones. These can go into soups and stews or really any dish you like. As a food group,

vegetables are versatile enough to be part of every meal or snack you eat. Creativity starts

with the veggie, and I have some inspiration for veggies from A to Z. Let's get started!

An artichoke is the bud of a flower. The flower in this case is a thistle. It has tough leaves on the outside with small thorns. These leaves cover the inside fuzzy middle, called the "choke," that sits atop the prize of the veggie, the "heart." The choke is not edible except in baby artichokes. You eat an artichoke from the outside-in, pulling the (trimmed) leaves through your teeth. Then you work your way through the leaves to that innermost delectable bite—the heart—and all the effort is well worth it. Here are a couple things you can do with artichokes.

Artichokes

Artichokes
with Lemon Balsamic Dipping Sauce
serves 4
45 minutes till it's ready

- 4 large artichokes
- 2 large lemons, 1 for artichokes and 3 tablespoons juice for sauce
- ½ cup mayonnaise
- ½ cup sour cream
- 1 tablespoon Dijon-style mustard
- 1 tablespoon white balsamic vinegar
- 1 tablespoon chopped fresh dill
- ½ teaspoon kosher salt
- ½ teaspoon coarse black pepper

1. Trim the first artichoke by first pulling off the thick dark-green outer leaves, leaving the tender green leaves in place. You'll lose about half of the leaves.
2. Use a vegetable peeler to trim the stem and remove the tough partial leaves from the bottom of the artichoke.
3. Cut off the tough end of the stem, leaving about 2 to 3 inches of tender stem.
4. Cut off the top third of the remaining artichoke leaves and discard.
5. With every slice or peel that you make, rub lemon over the cut ends.
6. Add each trimmed artichoke to a large pot with cold water and a few lemon slices while you trim the others.

7. Bring the artichokes to a boil over medium-high heat and cook until the tines of a fork can pierce the stem easily, about 30 to 45 minutes. Check after 15 minutes and add more water as it evaporates.
8. Stir together the mayonnaise, sour cream, Dijon mustard, lemon juice, vinegar, and fresh dill. Season with salt and pepper.
9. Transfer the artichokes to plates. Spoon on some of the sauce. Dredge the leaves of the artichoke into the sauce.
10. Once you have eaten most of the artichoke and are down to the most tender leaves, use a knife to separate the thorny choke from the artichoke bottom. Discard the spiky inner leaves and choke. Cut the heart into pieces and enjoy!

VIDEO: Trimming artichokes

Braised Baby Artichokes in Lemony Cream Sauce

serves 4 to 6

30 minutes till it's ready

- 1 (2 ½-pound) bag fresh baby artichokes, about 18
- 1 large lemon, 1 for artichokes and 2 tablespoons juice for sauce
- 2 tablespoons olive oil
- 4 large garlic cloves, peeled and minced, about 2 tablespoons
- 1 cup white wine
- 1 cup chicken stock
- 1 teaspoon dried oregano
- ½ cup sour cream
- 2 tablespoons chopped fresh parsley
- 1 teaspoon kosher salt
- ½ teaspoon coarse black pepper

1. Trim the dark outer leaves from the artichokes and discard. Trim the stems and cut off the pointed tips. Cut each one in half.
2. Add the trimmed artichokes to a bowl filled with cold water. Squeeze lemon wedges into the water to prevent the artichokes from discoloring.
3. Heat the olive oil in a skillet with a lid over medium-high. Cook the garlic until soft, about 3 to 4 minutes.
4. Add the artichokes.
5. Pour in the white wine and chicken stock. Stir in the oregano.
6. Reduce the heat to low. Cover and simmer until the artichokes are soft, about 10 to 15 minutes.
7. Remove the lid. Add the lemon juice and stir in the sour cream and parsley.
8. Season with salt and pepper.
9. Cook for 2 minutes more.

Thing to Note:
Once you learn how to trim a baby artichoke, you can easily incorporate this fun veggie into any of your dishes. Unlike its larger sibling, you do not need to remove the inside "choke"; baby artichokes are delicate enough to use thinly sliced in a salad. If you can't find fresh artichokes, frozen ones will do!

Fried Baby Artichokes

serves a bunch of friends
30 minutes till it's ready

- 10 to 12 baby artichokes, tough leaves trimmed
- 1 cup all-purpose flour
- 1 teaspoon kosher salt
- 1 teaspoon coarse black pepper
- 2 eggs, beaten with 2 tablespoons water
- 1 cup panko breadcrumbs
- olive oil for frying
- flaky sea salt

1. Cut the artichokes from top to stem into thin slices. A mandoline or handheld slicer is the perfect tool for this job.
2. Pour enough olive oil into a deep pot to come up halfway to the top. Heat over medium-high to 350°. (You can use a candy thermometer to check the temperature. Or you can add a drop of water to the hot oil. If it bubbles up, you're ready to fry!)
3. Dredge the slices first in the flour, then in the beaten eggs, and finally in the breadcrumbs.
4. Carefully place several slices of breaded artichoke into the hot oil. Cook until golden on one side, about 1 minute. Use a slotted spoon to carefully turn and cook on the second side until golden, about 1 to 2 minutes more.
5. Transfer to a baking sheet lined with paper towels. Season with flaky sea salt.
6. Serve warm with your favorite dipping sauce.

Thing to Note:
Need a sweet and spicy dipping sauce for your fried chokes? Here's one of my faves. For extra spice, add more hot sauce. For extra sweetness, up the ketchup content or add a bit of honey. Remember it's your sauce ... add whatever you want!

Sweet and Spicy Dipping Sauce

- ½ cup mayonnaise
- 2 tablespoons ketchup
- 2 tablespoons prepared horseradish
- 1 teaspoon paprika
- ½ teaspoon ground oregano
- 2 teaspoons kosher salt
- 1 teaspoon coarse black pepper
- 2 or more drops hot pepper sauce

1. Whisk together mayonnaise, ketchup, horseradish, paprika, and oregano.
2. Season with salt and pepper.
3. Stir in as much hot sauce as you like.
4. Pour the dipping sauce into a bowl.

Asparagus

When you're passing through the produce section of your grocery store looking for asparagus, you will find everything from pencil-thin spears to finger-thick stalks. If you're lucky enough to forage through a fresh market, you might find asparagus varieties that are white or even purple in color. Regardless of the color or size, asparagus is a delicious veggie that can be easily prepared. The spears have a tender tip and a woody, tough bottom. Bend your asparagus to figure out where the tougher part ends and snap it off! If the spear is thick, you might peel the darker part to reveal a light green stem. Here's a couple of recipe ideas to get you started.

Thing to Note:
To steam asparagus, place the spears into a steamer basket or metal colander that will fit into a larger pot. Add water to the pot, bring to a low boil, and cover. Steam the asparagus until the spears are tender.

Asparagus
with Hollandaise Sauce
serves 4
20 minutes till it's ready

- 8 large, thick asparagus spears, tough ends removed and bottom half peeled

For hollandaise sauce:
- 3 large egg yolks
- juice of 1 medium lemon, about 2 tablespoons
- ½ teaspoon dried tarragon
- ½ teaspoon kosher salt
- ⅛ teaspoon cayenne pepper
- ½ cup butter, 1 stick, melted

1. Steam the asparagus until the spears are just tender, about 2 to 4 minutes.
2. Add the egg yolks to a blender.
3. Add the lemon juice, tarragon, salt, and pepper.
4. Pulse to combine.
5. With the blender running on low speed, slowly drizzle in warm butter.
6. Continue mixing until the sauce becomes pale yellow and frothy-thick, just a couple of minutes.
7. Serve the asparagus with the sauce puddled over the top.

VIDEO: Peeling asparagus

You Can Cook Any THING
Peel Asparagus

White Asparagus in Cream

serves 4
20 minutes till it's ready

- 12 large, thick white asparagus spears, tough ends removed and bottom half peeled
- 2 tablespoons kosher salt
- ½ teaspoon granulated sugar
- 4 slices thick-sliced bacon, cut into small pieces
- 2 tablespoons butter
- 2 medium shallots, peeled and finely diced, about ½ cup
- ½ cup dry white wine
- ½ cup vegetable stock
- 1 cup heavy cream
- 2 tablespoons chopped fresh parsley

1. Bring a pot of water to boil. Add the salt and sugar.
2. Carefully drop the asparagus spears into the pot. Cook until they are tender, just a couple of minutes.
3. Transfer the spears to a platter, cover with aluminum foil to keep warm.
4. Fry the bacon in a sauté pan over medium-high heat until golden and crispy, about 5 minutes.
5. Use a slotted spoon to transfer the bacon pieces to paper towels to drain. Carefully pour out as much of the bacon fat as you can.
6. Add the butter to the pan and reduce the heat to medium.
7. Add the shallots and cook until soft, about 2 minutes.
8. Stir in vegetable stock and wine. Continue stirring, removing any bits from the bottom of the pan, until the liquid has almost completely disappeared.
9. Reduce the heat to medium.
10. Stir in the cream, half of the cooked bacon, and the parsley.
11. Cook until the sauce thickens and coats the back of a spoon, about 5 minutes.
12. Spoon the sauce over the asparagus. Garnish with the remaining bacon pieces and a bit more parsley.

Asparagus au Gratin
with Mushrooms and Shallots
serves 6
45 minutes till it's ready

- 14 large, thick asparagus spears, tough ends removed and bottom half peeled
- 4 tablespoons butter, divided
- 2 medium shallots, peeled and thinly sliced, about ½ cup
- 1 pint mushrooms, sliced, about 2 cups
- 1 teaspoon kosher salt
- ½ teaspoon coarse black pepper
- 2 tablespoons grated Parmesan cheese
- 2 tablespoons grated Gruyère cheese
- ½ cup heavy cream

1. Preheat your oven to 425°.
2. Coat a baking dish with vegetable oil spray. (If you have individual gratin dishes, this is the time to use them!)
3. Bring a pot of salted water to boil.
4. Prepare an ice bath.
5. Carefully drop the asparagus spears into the pot. Cook until tender, just a couple of minutes.
6. Transfer to the ice bath. Once the spears have cooled, drain them on paper towels.
7. Pat dry and cut them into 2-inch diagonal lengths.
8. Melt 2 tablespoons butter in a sauté pan over medium heat.
9. Add the shallots and mushrooms and cook until tender, about 2 to 4 minutes.
10. Season with salt and pepper.
11. Add the shallots and mushrooms to the bottom of the baking dish. Place the asparagus on top.
12. Cut the remaining butter into small pieces and scatter them around the dish.
13. Sprinkle on the cheese.
14. Pour the cream around the edges of the casserole.
15. Bake until golden and bubbling, about 25 to 30 minutes.

Thing to Note:
An ice water bath is a bowl of water filled with ice and topped off with water. If you plunge a cooked or partially cooked veggie right from the heat into an ice bath, the cooking process stops, and the veggie keeps its bright color. Pretty smart, huh?

Avocado

When you go to the grocery store, you'll probably see two different types of avocados. Florida avocados have smooth, green skin and tend to be larger than California (Hass) avocados. The difference is also found in the fat content. Hass have a deep, dark rippled green skin and the flesh is velvety and creamy. Both are excellent in recipes from guacamole to salads. You know the avocado is ripe when your fingers push into the skin and it gives just a bit. If it stays firm, place the avocado into a paper bag for a day or two to ripen it.

Avocado toasts are a great way to start your day. A terrific after-exercise, midmorning treat, a wonderful midday lunch, and a great midafternoon snack. I guess these toasts are just a great thing to have any darn time of the day!

Avocado Toasts
with Pickled Red Onion
serves 4
35 minutes till it's ready

For pickled onions:
- 1 medium red onion, peeled and thinly sliced, about 1 cup
- ½ cup red wine vinegar
- 1 tablespoon honey
- ½ teaspoon kosher salt

For toasts:
- 4 slices thick, crusty bread, toasted
- 4 (1-ounce) slices Swiss cheese
- 2 avocados, seeded
- juice of ½ lime, about 1 tablespoon
- 1 tablespoon olive oil
- ½ teaspoon coarse black pepper

1. Add the sliced onions to a bowl. Cover with vinegar and about ¼ cup warm water.
2. Stir in honey and season with a bit of salt.
3. Cover and let sit for 20 minutes. The onions will keep in the fridge for several days.
4. Place a slice of cheese on a warm slice of toasted bread.
5. Scoop the avocado flesh into a bowl. Add the lime juice and olive oil, and season with salt and pepper.
6. Use a fork to mash the avocado. Spread this onto the somewhat-melty cheese.
7. Drain a few strands of pickled onion from the liquid and lay them on the avocado.

Grilled Guac

makes about 2 to 3 cups guac
20 minutes till it's ready

Guacamole is a lovely mash-up of avocados and spice. I love it with chips and salsa, on my turkey sandwich, as a condiment for tacos, and of course it's a nacho necessity. Guac is pretty much perfect as is. But what happens when you take good old guacamole and kick the flavor up a notch? Well, try it and find out!

- 2 tablespoons olive oil
- 2 medium ripe avocados, pit removed
- 4 medium plum tomatoes, halved
- ½ large red onion, peeled and cut into ½-inch rounds
- 2 large jalapeño peppers, cut in half and seeded
- 2 limes, cut in half
- 6 cloves roasted garlic
- 1 teaspoon ground chili powder
- 1 teaspoon kosher salt
- ½ teaspoon coarse ground pepper

1. Heat a grill pan over high heat.
2. Drizzle with 2 tablespoons olive oil.
3. Lay the avocado, tomatoes, onion, jalapeño peppers, and limes onto the grill pan, cut side down. Cook until you see grill marks, about 3 to 5 minutes. Flip everything and cook for about 2 to 3 minutes more. You want the onions to be fork tender and the rest of the food firm, but not mushy.
4. Transfer everything to your work surface and let cool.
5. Scoop the flesh from the avocado into a bowl.
6. Chop and add the tomatoes, onion, and jalapeños.
7. Squeeze the juice of one lime into the bowl.
8. Add the roasted garlic.
9. Season with chili powder, salt, and pepper.
10. Use a potato masher to combine to your desired consistency. The longer you mash, the smoother it will become.
11. You can drizzle more olive oil into the mixture for added richness and more lime juice for extra smoothness.

VIDEO: Making grilled guac

Avocado Soup
with Spinach and Dill
serves 6 to 8
45 minutes till it's ready

- 2 tablespoons olive oil
- 1 large yellow onion, peeled and diced, about 1 ½ cup
- 3 to 4 garlic cloves, peeled and sliced, about 2 tablespoons
- 1 small jalapeño pepper, seeded and diced, about 2 tablespoons
- 3 medium baking potatoes, peeled and diced, about 3 cups
- 2 quarts chicken stock
- 1 pound fresh spinach leaves, about 4 to 5 cups
- 2 medium Hass avocados or 1 larger Florida avocado, pitted, peeled, and diced, about 3 cups
- 2 tablespoons chopped fresh dill
- 1 teaspoon kosher salt
- ½ teaspoon coarse black pepper

1. Heat olive oil in a large pot over medium-high heat.
2. Add the onion and cook until soft and translucent, about 5 minutes.
3. Add the garlic and jalapeño and cook 2 to 3 minutes more.
4. Add the potatoes and stir.
5. Pour in the chicken stock.
6. Reduce the heat to medium and simmer until the potatoes are tender, about 15 minutes.
7. Add the spinach leaves one handful at a time, until cooked down.
8. Add the avocado and dill and turn off the heat.
9. Cool the soup to room temperature. (Watch out here. Hot soup will expand when blended and pop the top off your blender!)
10. Use a blender, food processor, or handheld immersion blender to puree the soup until smooth and velvety.
11. Pour back into the pot and season with salt and pepper.
12. You can serve the soup warm or chill it in the fridge to serve cold.
13. Garnish the soup with toasted pine nuts, a dollop of sour cream, crunchy croutons, or a grilled shrimp. You can garnish this soup with just about anything!

Soup's on! Avocado soup, that is. Easy to prepare and adaptable to serve, this soup will become one of your favorites.

Green Beans

Fresh beans are a snap to prepare, which makes them perfect for weekend meals. Speaking of snap, that's how you can tell that the beans you've chosen are fresh. Pick beans that are deep green in color, tender, long, and crisp, but flexible. When you break the bean in half, you want to hear a crisp snapping sound. Here's a couple ideas for your next snappin' fresh side dish.

Chilled Green Bean and Arugula Salad
with Mustard Shallot Vinaigrette and Chopped Egg
serves 6
45 minutes till it's ready

- 1 pound fresh green beans, trimmed, about 3 cups
- 3 cups loosely packed arugula leaves, torn into bite-size pieces

For vinaigrette:
- 1 medium shallot, peeled and finely diced, about ¼ cup
- ½ cup white balsamic vinegar
- 1 tablespoon Dijon-style mustard
- 1 teaspoon honey
- 1 cup olive oil
- 1 tablespoon chopped fresh mint
- 1 teaspoon salt
- ½ teaspoon coarse black pepper

For eggs:
- 2 large eggs, hard boiled, peeled, and diced
- 1 tablespoon mayonnaise
- 4 slices bacon, cooked and crumbled

1. Cut the beans into 2-inch pieces.
2. Blanch in boiling salted water and transfer to an ice bath to stop the cooking process. Drain and pat dry.
3. Toss the green beans with the arugula in a bowl and place into the fridge to chill.
4. Add the shallot into a small bowl.
5. Add the vinegar, mustard, and honey. Slowly whisk in the olive oil.
6. Stir in the mint and season with some of the salt and pepper.
7. Stir the mayonnaise into the diced egg. Season with some of the salt and pepper.
8. Pour some of the vinaigrette over the green bean salad and toss. You want to lightly coat the ingredients, not drown them!
9. Create a well in the middle of the salad. Scoop the egg salad into the well.
10. Top with crumbled bacon.

VIDEO: Making soft and jammy hard-boiled eggs

Super Soft Green Beans
with Caramelized Onions
serves 4 to 6
20 minutes till it's ready

For onions:
- 1 (10-ounce) bag pearl onions, about 2 ½ to 3 dozen
- 3 tablespoons butter
- 3 tablespoons brown sugar
- 1 tablespoon balsamic vinegar
- 1 teaspoon kosher salt
- ½ teaspoon coarse black pepper

For the green beans:
- 1 tablespoon olive oil
- 1 tablespoon butter
- 2 garlic cloves, peeled and minced, about 1 tablespoon
- 1 pound green beans, ends trimmed, about 3 cups
- 1 ½ cups chicken stock

1. Add the peeled onions to a skillet and cover with water.
2. Bring to a boil over high heat and cook for 10 minutes.
3. Add 3 tablespoons butter and the brown sugar and vinegar.
4. Continue cooking until most of the liquid has evaporated and the onions are tender, browned, and syrupy, about 10 minutes more.
5. Season with some of the salt and pepper.
6. Note that you can prep the onions in advance. Store in an airtight container in the fridge and heat them when you are ready to serve.
7. Heat the olive oil and 1 tablespoon butter in a sauté pan with a lid over medium heat.
8. Add the garlic and green beans. Season with salt and pepper.
9. Pour in the chicken stock.
10. Cover the pan with the lid and simmer the beans until they are quite soft, about 20 to 30 minutes.
11. Use a slotted spoon to transfer the beans to a serving bowl.
12. Increase the heat and bring the remaining liquid to a boil. Cook until the liquid has reduced by half, about 5 minutes.
13. Pour the liquid over the beans.
14. Spoon the caramelized onions on top.

Thing to Note:
To peel pearl onions, cut a slit in the root bottom of each one. Boil for two minutes. Transfer to an ice bath. Pinch the skins to pop out the onion.

VIDEO: Peeling and cooking pearl onions

You Can Cook Any THING

PRIVACY.FLOWCODE.COM

Pearl Onions

Farmers Market Minestrone

serves a crowd
45 minutes to prep, plus a bit more for simmering

- 2 tablespoons olive oil
- 4 to 5 links Italian sausage, sliced into ½-inch circles
- ⅔ pound green beans, trimmed, about 2 cups
- 2 to 3 large carrots, peeled and diced, about 2 cups
- 1 large onion, peeled and diced, about 1 ½ cups
- 1 medium zucchini, diced, about 1 cup
- 2 small poblano peppers, seeded and deveined, diced, about 1 cup
- 6 large garlic cloves, peeled and diced, about ¼ cup

- 1 (28-ounce) can diced tomatoes
- 4 cups beef stock
- 2 tablespoons dried oregano
- 2 teaspoons kosher salt
- 2 teaspoons coarse black pepper
- outer rind of 2-inch piece of Parmesan cheese
- ½ pound kale, stems chopped, leaves rolled and chopped, about 4 cups
- Parmesan cheese, grated
- chopped fresh basil leaves
- 12 ounces small elbow macaroni

1. Heat olive oil in a deep pot over medium heat.
2. Add the sausage and brown on all sides, about 5 minutes. Remove the sausage.
3. Add the green beans, carrots, onion, and zucchini to the pot. Cook until the veggies are soft and beginning to brown, about 10 to 15 minutes.
4. Add the peppers and garlic. Cook for 5 minutes more.
5. Pour in the tomatoes and beef stock. Season with oregano, salt, and pepper. Bring the soup to a simmer.
6. Add the sausage back to the pot. Submerge the cheese rind in the soup. Stir in the kale.
7. Add water to the pot to make sure that all the ingredients are covered in liquid.
8. Continue to simmer until the kale wilts and the cheese has melted, at least 45 minutes and up to several hours on the stove over low heat. You can add more water as needed.
9. Continue to taste the soup and season with salt and pepper as needed.
10. Add the macaroni and continue to simmer while the pasta cooks in the soup. When the pasta is plump and soft, the soup is ready!
11. Serve the soup with a garnish of grated Parmesan cheese and a sprinkle of fresh basil on top.

Thing to Note:
Submerging a rind of Parmesan cheese will slightly thicken the broth and infuse it with a cheesy depth of flavor.

VIDEO: Making beef stock

You Can Cook Any THING
How To Make Beef Stock

Beets are a bit messy to work with, which may make you weary of using them. But trust me, beets are well worth the cleanup! Once you have made up your mind to get your hands a little dirty, you will find there are lots of things to do with beets. Here are a couple of ideas.

Citrus Marinated Beets

serves 4 to 6
20 minutes, plus marinating overnight,
till it's ready

- 6 (2- to 3-inch diameter) beets
- zest of ½ medium orange, about 1 tablespoon
- juice of ½ medium orange,
  about 2 to 3 tablespoons
- 1 tablespoon red wine vinegar
- 1 tablespoon olive oil
- 1 tablespoon chopped fresh mint
- 1 teaspoon kosher salt
- ½ teaspoon coarse black pepper

1. Preheat oven to 375°.
2. Wash the beets. Cut the bottom and top shoots from each beet and discard.
3. Add the beets to a casserole dish with lid. Pour about ½ inch of water in the bottom of the dish.
4. Cover and cook until the beets begin to soften, about 40 to 45 minutes. (The beets will not be as soft as a cooked potato; however, you will be able to insert the tip of a sharp knife without much resistance.) Cool the beets to room temperature.
5. Peel the beets and cut into thin slices.
6. Add the sliced beets to a bowl.
7. Sprinkle with orange zest and pour in orange juice, vinegar, and olive oil. Add chopped fresh mint, salt, and pepper. Toss to coat.
8. Cover the dish and chill the beets overnight.

Beets

Thing to Note:
While peeling beets it's easy to stain your skin— and that doesn't come out easily. To get around this, use paper towels to remove the skin. It's still messy, but not as bad!

Make it "My Way":
Season your beets! Heat olive oil in a skillet over medium high. Add your favorite spice combination. (I like a combination of ground cinnamon, nutmeg, brown sugar, cumin, and chili powder.) Toss to coat. Cook for 5 to 10 minutes until the beets are seasoned and warmed through.

VIDEO: Roasting beets

Roast Beets

Sautéed Beets and Spinach
serves 4 to 6
30 minutes until it's ready

- 2 tablespoons butter
- 1 large shallot, peeled and thinly sliced, about 2 tablespoons
- 6 to 8 medium beets, scrubbed, peeled, and sliced into ¼-inch disks
- ½ pound fresh spinach leaves chopped, about 2 cups
- 1 teaspoon coarse salt
- ½ teaspoon coarse ground pepper
- 1 cup chicken broth

1. Melt the butter in a large sauté pan over medium high heat.
2. Add the shallot and cook until soft, about 2 minutes.
3. Add the beets, reduce the heat to medium, and simmer until soft, about 15 minutes.
4. Add the spinach and pour in the chicken broth. Simmer until the veggies are soft and most of the liquid has been absorbed, about 5 minutes more.
5. Season with salt and pepper.

How many times have you heard (or have you said) "Eat your broccoli"? Probably at least once! Why? Because broccoli is an easy, quick veggie to prepare and checks all the nutrition boxes at dinner time. Like chicken, broccoli is an empty canvas just waiting for you to season and sauce it up. Here's what I mean.

Broccoli

Broccoli
a Couple of Ways
serves 2 to 4
about 20 minutes per recipe

- 1 head broccoli, cut into florets, about 3 ½ cups
- 6 tablespoons butter, divided
- 1 teaspoon kosher salt
- ½ teaspoon coarse black pepper
- 2 medium garlic cloves, minced, about 1 tablespoon
- ½ cup seasoned breadcrumbs
- 1 large egg, hard-boiled and finely chopped
- 1 tablespoon chopped fresh cilantro

1. Preheat your oven to 350°.
2. Prepare an ice bath.
3. Cut the broccoli into 2-inch pieces. Blanch in boiling water for 4 to 5 minutes or until bright green.
4. Transfer to ice bath. Drain through a colander.
5. Melt 2 tablespoons butter. Place the broccoli into a baking dish. Toss with melted butter and season with salt and pepper. Bake for 10 minutes.
6. Melt the remaining 4 tablespoons butter in a skillet over medium-high heat.
7. Cook the garlic in the butter for 2 minutes.
8. Add the breadcrumbs and cook until they turn brown and begin to crisp, about 4 minutes. Season with salt and pepper.
9. Remove the broccoli from the oven. Spoon the breadcrumbs over the top. Garnish with chopped hard-boiled egg and cilantro.

Make it "My Way":
Sautéed Broccoli with Lemon

Blanch the broccoli and drain. Heat 2 tablespoons olive oil in a skillet over medium-high heat. Add 2 minced garlic cloves. Add the broccoli to the skillet. Pour in the juice of 1 lemon. Season with salt and freshly ground pepper.

Broccoli with Ginger Sauce

Blanch broccoli and drain. Melt 2 tablespoons butter in a skillet over medium-high heat. Add 1 teaspoon freshly minced ginger. Add the broccoli to the skillet. Pour in 1 tablespoon soy sauce and sprinkle with 1 tablespoon sesame seeds. Season with freshly ground pepper.

VIDEO: Blanching veggies

Broccoli Rabe
with Garlic, Lemon, and Red Pepper
serves 4 to 6
20 minutes till it's ready

- 1 large bunch broccoli rabe, chopped, about 4 cups
- 1 teaspoon kosher salt
- ½ teaspoon coarse black pepper
- 2 tablespoons olive oil
- 6 medium garlic cloves, thinly sliced, about ¼ cup
- ¼ teaspoon red pepper flakes
- juice of 1 medium lemon, about 2 tablespoons
- ½ teaspoon coarse black pepper

1. Bring a pot of water to boil over high heat.
2. Season with salt.
3. Prepare an ice bath.
4. Cut the tough stems from the broccoli rabe.
5. Chop the stalks into 1-inch pieces. Roughly chop the leaves.
6. Add the stems to the pot and cook until just tender, about 5 minutes. Add the leaves and cook for 3 to 5 minutes more. Drain the broccoli rabe using a colander.
7. Plunge the greens into an ice bath to stop the cooking process. Drain again.
8. Heat the olive oil in a skillet over medium-low.
9. Add the garlic and red pepper flakes to the skillet and cook until just golden, about 1 to 2 minutes.
10. Add the blanched broccoli rabe to the pan and toss.
11. Sprinkle with lemon juice and season with salt and pepper.

Make it "My Way":
Once you have mastered broccoli-rabe making, try one of these awesome recipes:

Pasta with Broccoli Rabe, Sun-dried Tomatoes, and Fresh Mozzarella

Cook your pasta according to package directions. Combine blanched broccoli rabe, sun-dried tomatoes cut into strips, and cubes of fresh mozzarella in a serving bowl. Drain pasta and add to the mix. Toss until the mozzarella has just begun to melt. Season with salt, pepper, and shavings of Parmesan.

Lasagna with Broccoli Rabe

Prepare your lasagna noodles. Mix ricotta cheese with cooked and chopped broccoli rabe. (I add an egg and Parmesan to this mixture, which adds richness.) Plop generous spoonfuls of the ricotta mixture onto the noodles, cover with tomato sauce, and sprinkle with cheese. Continue layering for a red, white, and green treat.

Brussels Sprouts

Once the villains of veggie world, these sprouts have rebranded themselves and become a trendy restaurant fave. I truly think the sprouts you find in the grocery store are prettier than they used to be. I don't know how that happened, but it seems to me like this veggie has had a movie-star makeover. I do have a secret when preparing Brussels sprouts: I blanch them first before I roast or sauté. This ensures that the inside is tender, and that's what you want. No one likes to eat something that is rock hard. Here's a couple of my favorite recipes that incorporate sprouts.

Roasted-Veggie Winter Salad
with Meyer Lemon–Basil Vinaigrette
serves a crowd
45 minutes till it's ready

For roasted vegetables:
- 3 whole beets, trimmed
- 1 teaspoon kosher salt
- 1 teaspoon coarse black pepper
- 2 tablespoons olive oil
- 2 tablespoons Dijon-style mustard
- 2 ounces Parmesan cheese, grated, about ½ cup
- 6 medium carrots, tops removed, peeled, and cut into 1-inch pieces
- 12 new potatoes, cut into fourths
- 12 Brussels sprouts, cut in half
- 1 small butternut squash, peeled and cut into 1-inch cubes, about 2 to 3 cups

1. Preheat your oven to 400°.
2. Wrap the beets in aluminum foil and place into the oven. Roast the beets until soft, about 45 minutes.
3. Drizzle 2 tablespoons olive oil into a large baking sheet with rim. Smear the mustard into the bottom of the baking sheet. Add the Parmesan cheese.
4. Add the carrots into a microwave-safe bowl. Add 2 tablespoons water. Cover the bowl with plastic wrap. Microwave on high for 4 minutes.
5. Drain the carrots and arrange on the baking sheet.
6. Repeat the same process, microwaving the potatoes, Brussels sprouts, and butternut squash. We're giving the veggies a head start for the roasting process.

For salad:
- 1 small shallot, peeled and minced, about 2 tablespoons
- 1 tablespoon Dijon-style mustard
- juice of 1 large Meyer lemon, about ¼ cup
- ¼ cup white balsamic vinegar
- 1 tablespoon honey
- ½ cup olive oil
- 2 tablespoons chopped fresh basil
- 6 cups mixed lettuce leaves
- 2 ounces Gorgonzola cheese, crumbled, about ½ cup

7. Use your hands to coat the veggies with the seasonings in the bottom of the baking sheet. Season with some of the salt and pepper.
8. Roast until the vegetables are just beginning to turn golden, about 12 to 15 minutes. You can use a spatula to flip the veggies about halfway through cooking, if you like, but it's not necessary.
9. Remove the beets from the oven and cool to room temperature. Peel the beets and cut into 1-inch pieces. Season with salt and pepper and set aside.
10. Place the shallots into a small bowl. Add the Dijon mustard, lemon juice, balsamic vinegar, and honey. Drizzle in the oil, whisking to combine. Taste and season with salt and pepper. Whisk in the basil.
11. Lay the lettuce into a shallow bowl. Pour just enough vinaigrette over the leaves to moisten them. (Don't drown your lettuce!)
12. Place the roasted veggies on top of the lettuce. Sprinkle the cheese over top. Drizzle a little more vinaigrette over the top.

Sheet Pan Roasted Veggies
serves a crowd
45 minutes till it's ready

- 16 to 20 Brussels sprouts
- 2 tablespoons balsamic vinegar
- juice of ½ medium lemon, about 2 tablespoons
- 1 tablespoon olive oil, plus more for the other veggies
- 1 teaspoon kosher salt, plus more for the other veggies
- ½ teaspoon coarse black pepper, plus more for the other veggies
- 1 large head cauliflower, cut into 1-inch florets, about 5 to 6 cups

- 2 tablespoons Dijon-style mustard
- 2 tablespoons grated Parmesan cheese
- 2 garlic cloves, minced, about 2 teaspoons
- 1 teaspoon dried thyme
- 16 to 20 whole baby carrots
- 2 tablespoons brown sugar
- 1 teaspoon ground curry powder
- 16 to 20 asparagus spears
- 2 tablespoons mayonnaise
- 2 large yellow onions
- 1 large fennel bulb

1. Preheat your oven to 425°.
2. Cut each Brussels sprout in half and steam (or blanch) until they begin to soften, about 4 to 5 minutes.
3. Toss with balsamic vinegar, lemon juice, olive oil, salt, and pepper. Transfer to a baking sheet.
4. Toss the cauliflower with mustard, Parmesan cheese, garlic, thyme, olive oil, salt, and pepper. Transfer to the baking sheet.
5. Toss the carrots with brown sugar, curry powder, olive oil, salt, and pepper. Transfer to the baking sheet.
6. Toss the asparagus with mayonnaise, olive oil, salt, and pepper. Transfer to the baking sheet.
7. Cut the onion into wedges, leaving the root intact. This will help to keep the onion together. Toss with olive oil, salt, and pepper. Transfer to the baking sheet.
8. Remove the tops and tough core from the fennel bulb and cut into thick slices. Season with olive oil, salt, and pepper. Transfer to the baking sheet.
9. You can prepare the vegetables to this point several hours in advance and stick the pan in the fridge. When you are ready to serve, roast the veggies until they begin to crisp and brown, about 20 minutes.
10. You can serve them warm or at room temperature.

Cabbage

Cabbage is a kind of cousin to broccoli. It is wonderful when shredded into coleslaw or terrific when fermented into sauerkraut. I like it as a side with pork. Somehow, they pair just right. I also like to add other veggies and fruits to the cabbage to liven things up. Here's what I mean.

Savoy Cabbage
with Fennel and Apples
serves 4 to 6
40 minutes till it's ready

- 1 (2-pound) head savoy cabbage
- 2 tablespoons butter
- 2 tablespoons olive oil
- 1 medium yellow onion, diced, about 1 ½ cups
- 1 medium fennel bulb, diced, about 1 cup
- 2 medium apples, peeled and thinly sliced, about 2 cups
- 1 cup apple cider
- 2 cups chicken stock
- 1 teaspoon kosher salt
- ½ teaspoon ground pepper
- ½ teaspoon ground cardamom
- ½ teaspoon ground cinnamon

1. Cut the cabbage into thin slices.
2. Melt the butter with the olive oil in a large sauté pan with lid over medium heat.
3. Add the onion and fennel and cook until soft, about 5 minutes.
4. Add the cabbage and cook for 10 minutes.
5. Stir in the apples.
6. Pour in the cider.
7. Cook until very little liquid remains, about 5 minutes more.
8. Add the chicken stock and season with salt and pepper, cardamom, and cinnamon.
9. Cover and simmer until soft, about 30 minutes.

Thing to Note:
If you want to throw a couple of carrots or sliced onions into the baking dish with the cauliflower and garlic, feel free! They'll work great here.

Stuffed Cabbage Rolls

serves 6 to 8, about 10 to 12 (3-inch) rolls
about 30 minutes prep, plus 1 hour to bake

For sauce:
- 1 tablespoon olive oil
- 1 medium white onion, diced, about ⅔ cup
- 2 tablespoons paprika
- 2 tablespoons tomato paste
- 1 (28-ounce) can diced tomatoes
- 1 cup chicken broth
- 2 tablespoons brown sugar
- 2 tablespoons balsamic vinegar
- 1 tablespoon chopped fresh sage
- 1 cup raisins

For rolls:
- 1 whole cabbage
- 1 pound ground beef (substitute with ground turkey or pork or a combo of all 3)
- 1 teaspoon kosher salt
- 1 teaspoon coarse black pepper
- 1 teaspoon dried minced onion
- 1 teaspoon garlic powder
- 1 teaspoon paprika
- 2 cups cooked white rice
- 2 tablespoons chopped fresh parsley

1. Prepare the sauce by heating 1 tablespoon olive oil in a saucepot over medium-high heat.
2. Cook the white onion until soft.
3. Add 2 tablespoons paprika and tomato paste.
4. Cook for 2 to 3 minutes.
5. Add the diced tomatoes, chicken broth, brown sugar, balsamic vinegar, raisins, and sage.
6. Simmer for 5 to 10 minutes.
7. Season with salt and pepper.
8. Heat a large pot of water to boiling over high heat.
9. Prepare ice bath.
10. Cut the stem and the core from the cabbage. Plunge the cabbage into the water. Cook in the boiling water for 5 minutes.
11. Remove the whole cabbage from the pot and plunge into the ice water. When cool enough to handle, gently remove the outer leaves.
12. Pat the leaves dry. Continue until you have removed 10 to 12 leaves. Save the remaining cabbage for another use.
13. Place the beef into a bowl. Season with salt, pepper, minced onion, garlic powder, and 1 teaspoon paprika.
14. Stir in the cooked rice and parsley.
15. Place ⅓ cup meat filling on the bottom stem part of a cabbage leaf, leaving about a 1-inch border. Wrap the leaf from stem border over the filling. Fold in the sides. Continue wrapping until you have used all the leaves and filling.
16. Preheat the oven to 375°. Place 1 cup of the sauce into the bottom of a baking dish or Dutch oven.
17. Place the stuffed cabbage in a single layer into the dish. Cover with the remaining sauce.
18. Cover the pot and bake until the meat in the center is cooked through (reaching an internal temperature of 160°).

VIDEO: Making stuffed cabbage rolls

Sure, you can dice them, shave them, slice them, or julienne them—but you can also find them pre-cut or sliced, ready to grab and use without a second thought. There's not a week that goes by that I'm not roasting a carrot or sautéing it for a sauce or stew. Next is a special preparation that goes back years and years for me. My mom used to make this at Thanksgiving. This dish is literally like having your cake and eating it too.

Carrots

Carrot Ring
with Creamed Pearl Onions and Peas
serves a crowd
20 minutes to pull together
and 60 minutes to bake

- 1 tablespoon olive oil
- 2 tablespoons breadcrumbs
- 4 large eggs, separated
- ¾ pound butter, 3 sticks, room temperature
- 1 cup granulated sugar
- 6 large carrots, peeled and grated, about 3 cups
- 2 tablespoons milk
- juice of 1 medium lemon, about 2 tablespoons
- 1 teaspoon kosher salt
- 2 teaspoons baking powder
- 1 teaspoon baking soda
- 2 cups unbleached all-purpose flour
- 1 (9-ounce) package frozen pearl onions in cream sauce, thawed
- 1 (9-ounce) package frozen sweet peas, thawed

1. Preheat your oven to 350°.
2. Brush a 10-inch Bundt or tube pan with olive oil.
3. Dust the bottom and sides of the pan evenly with breadcrumbs.
4. Use an electric mixer fitted with the whisk attachment to beat the egg whites until stiff peaks form. Transfer the egg whites to another bowl and set aside.
5. Use the electric mixer fitted with a paddle attachment to mix the butter and the sugar until creamy.
6. Stir in the egg yolks one at time.
7. Add carrots, milk, and lemon juice and beat until well mixed.

8. Add salt, baking powder, baking soda, and flour and beat again until well mixed.
9. Remove the bowl and use a spatula to fold in the beaten egg whites until no white streaks remain. Pour the batter into the prepared pan.
10. Bake until golden brown and the top springs back when touched, about one hour.
11. Remove from the oven and let cool for about 5 minutes.
12. Use a knife to loosen the sides of the cake and remove it from the pan, turning it, bottom side up, onto a serving platter.
13. Warm the onions and peas in a saucepot over medium heat. Spoon the veggies into the center of the mold and over the sides.
14. Cut the carrot ring into slices and serve warm.

VIDEO: Folding ingredients

Classic Cabbage and Carrot Coleslaw

serves 6 to 8

20 minutes till it's ready

- 1 (2-pound) head green cabbage, shredded, about 6 to 8 cups
- 2 large carrots, shredded, about 1 cup
- ½ cup mayonnaise
- 2 tablespoons tarragon vinegar
- 1 tablespoon granulated sugar
- 1 teaspoon celery seed
- 1 teaspoon kosher salt
- ½ teaspoon coarse black pepper
- 2 tablespoons chopped fresh parsley

1. Place the shredded cabbage and carrots into a large bowl. Stir together the mayonnaise, vinegar, sugar, and celery seed. Season with salt and pepper.
2. Pour the sauce over the cabbage and toss to coat.
3. Cover and refrigerate for at least 1 hour.
4. Garnish with fresh chopped parsley.

Thing to Note:

For this recipe you can easily take advantage of the prepackaged, preshredded veggies that are in the produce section in the grocery store. Shredded broccoli and purple cabbage are great additions. Others include shredded bell peppers and a touch of sliced onion. For a Mexican spin on traditional coleslaw, add thin strips of seeded jalapeño pepper, a sprinkle of lime juice, and a dash of ground cumin. Garnish with fresh cilantro instead of parsley.

Cauliflower

Garlic-Roasted Cauliflower
in Cheesy Sauce
serves 4 to 6
20 minutes, plus about 30 minutes
to roast, till it's ready

Cauliflower is versatile—so versatile that it is used as a look-alike rice and as a base for pizza crust. Here are a couple of more things you can do with cauliflower.

For cauliflower:
- 1 large head cauliflower, cut into 1-inch florets, about 5 to 6 cups
- 1 head garlic, cloves peeled and thinly sliced, about ½ cup
- 2 tablespoons olive oil
- 1 teaspoon ground paprika
- 1 teaspoon kosher salt
- ½ teaspoon coarse black pepper

For cheese sauce:
- 2 tablespoons butter
- 2 tablespoons flour
- 2 cups milk
- ½ teaspoon ground nutmeg
- 4 ounces cheddar cheese, grated, about 1 cup
- 2 ounces Parmesan cheese, finely grated, about ½ cup

1. Preheat your oven to 350°.
2. Add the florets to a baking dish. Toss in the garlic cloves. Drizzle with olive oil. Sprinkle with paprika. Season with salt and pepper.
3. Cook until the cauliflower is tender, about 10 to 15 minutes.
4. Heat the butter in a deep pot over medium-high heat.
5. Whisk in the flour. Cook until golden and bubbling, about 2 to 4 minutes.
6. Pour in the milk. Cook, stirring constantly until the sauce is thickened, about 6 to 8 minutes. Season with salt, pepper, and nutmeg.
7. Remove the sauce from the heat and stir in the cheese until melted.
8. Remove the baking dish from the oven.
9. Pour the cheese sauce over the cauliflower. Sprinkle with Parmesan cheese.
10. Place the baking dish back into the oven and bake until the sauce begins to brown and bubble, about 5 minutes more.

Crispy Cauliflower
with Buffalo Sauce
serves 4 to 6

30 minutes till it's ready

- oil for frying
- ½ cup cornstarch
- ½ cup unbleached all-purpose flour
- ½ teaspoon baking powder
- ½ teaspoon kosher salt
- ½ cup vodka

- 1 head cauliflower, cut into 1-inch florets, about 4 to 5 cups
- 2 to 4 garlic cloves, peeled and minced
- 2 tablespoons butter, melted
- ¼ cup hot pepper sauce
- 2 tablespoons chopped fresh chives

1. Add oil to a deep pot coming up no more than ⅓ of the side. Heat to 375°.
2. Whisk together the cornstarch, flour, baking powder, and salt with vodka and ½ cup water in a large bowl to make a thin batter, with a consistency like cream.
3. Place the cauliflower into the bowl and toss to coat.
4. Add cauliflower pieces to the oil. Do not overcrowd the pot. Cook until the cauliflower turns golden brown, about 3 to 5 minutes. Transfer to a paper-towel lined baking sheet.
5. In a large bowl, mix the garlic and butter. Stir in the hot pepper sauce.
6. Toss the fried cauliflower in the sauce. Transfer to a serving platter and garnish with chopped chives.

VIDEO: Frying cauliflower

Corn

When I prepare corn, I purposefully make more than I need (surprise, surprise!) because I like to use the leftovers in other veggie side dishes. Remove the kernels from the cob and store them in an airtight container. When you are ready, you can sauté them in oil with other veggies a la succotash. You can also toast them in a fry pan and blend them with black beans, tomatoes, chilis, and cilantro for a yummy salsa—or you can turn them into a delicious salad, like this one.

Grilled Corn Salad
With Lemon-Basil Vinaigrette
serves a crowd
20 minutes till it's ready

For salad:
- 6 ears of corn
- 1 English cucumber, cut into ½-inch chunks, about 2 cups
- 1 bunch green onions, diced, about ½ cup
- 1 pint cherry tomatoes, halved, about 2 cups

For vinaigrette:
- 1 bunch basil leaves, about 1 cup
- 1 tablespoon Dijon-style mustard
- juice of 1 large lemon, about 3 tablespoons
- ¼ cup white balsamic vinegar
- 1 tablespoon honey
- ½ cup olive oil
- 1 teaspoon kosher salt
- ½ teaspoon coarse black pepper
- 2 ounces Parmesan cheese, shaved, about ½ cup

1. Remove the husks from the corn and grill over medium heat, turning often, until the kernels are golden brown. Cool to room temperature.
2. Cut the kernels from the cobs into a bowl.
3. Add the cucumber, green onions, and cherry tomatoes.
4. Add the basil leaves into a blender or the bowl of a food processor. Add the mustard, lemon juice, balsamic vinegar, and honey. Pulse to combine.
5. With the machine running, slowly pour in the olive oil. Season with salt and pepper.
6. Drizzle some of the dressing over the corn salad. Toss to just coat the veggies. You want just a bit of dressing; you don't want it to be soggy.
7. Garnish with shaved Parmesan cheese.

Creamed Corn

serves 6 to 8
90 minute cuisine

- 6 large ears of corn, husks removed
- 2 ½ cups heavy whipping cream
- 2 teaspoons kosher salt
- 4 slices bacon, diced
- 1 small yellow onion, peeled and diced, about ½ cup
- 1 small red bell pepper, seeded, deveined, and diced, about ½ cup
- 1 medium jalapeño pepper, seeded, deveined, and finely diced, about 1 tablespoon
- 4 large garlic cloves, peeled and minced
- 2 to 3 green onions, thinly sliced
- 1 teaspoon coarse black pepper

1. Cut the kernels from the cobs into a bowl.
2. Break the bare cobs in half and add to a deep pot. Pour in the cream and season with 1 teaspoon of salt.
3. Cover the pot and cook over medium-high heat until the cream begins to boil.
4. Turn off the heat and steep the cobs in the cream for 1 hour.
5. Use a spoon to scrape the pulp from each cob piece and add back to the cream. Discard cobs.
6. Cook the bacon in a large sauté pan over medium heat until crisp. Remove the bacon and rest on paper towels to drain.
7. Add the onion and peppers and cook for 2 to 3 minutes.
8. Stir in the garlic and cook for 1 minute more.
9. Add the corn and ¾ of the cream.
10. Reduce the heat to low and simmer until the corn is soft and tender, about 20 to 30 minutes.
11. Stir in the rest of the cream and half of the green onions and bacon. Season with salt and pepper.
12. Garnish with the remaining green onions and bacon on top!

Cucumbers

When you buy a cucumber in the grocery store, you have a couple of choices. I usually pick an English (or hot house) cucumber because these have fewer seeds, making them perfect for salads. They also come in a miniature form, which are terrific for pickling. Once they're pickled, they are even better fried. Take a look!

Fried Pickles
with Spicy Dipping Sauce
serves a crowd
30 minutes till it's ready

For Sauce:
- ½ cup mayonnaise
- 2 tablespoons chili sauce
- 2 tablespoons hot pepper sauce
- 1 tablespoon Worcestershire sauce
- 1 teaspoon garlic powder
- ½ teaspoon kosher salt
- ½ teaspoon coarse black pepper

For Pickles:
- 1 large jar whole dill pickles, drained
- ½ cup all-purpose flour
- 1 teaspoon Italian seasoning
- 1 teaspoon garlic powder
- 1 teaspoon kosher salt
- ½ cup buttermilk
- vegetable (or peanut) oil for frying

1. Whisk together the sauce ingredients in a small bowl. Set aside while you fry the pickles.
2. Cut the pickles into ¼-inch thick diagonal slices.
3. Lay the slices on a baking sheet lined with paper towels. Use more paper towels to dry the pickle slices thoroughly. Place the pickles into the fridge while you stir together the sauce.
4. Place the flour, Italian seasoning, and garlic powder in a bowl. Stir in the buttermilk. Season with salt and pepper. The batter will be thick.
5. Heat vegetable oil (to about 375°) in a fryer or deep pot over high heat. You want enough oil to only come up ⅓ of the side of the pan.
6. Dip one pickle slice into the batter. Shake off excess and carefully place in the hot oil. Repeat with several pickle slices. Do not overcrowd the pan.
7. Use a slotted spoon to turn the pickles slices over once they are golden on one side, about 1 to 2 minutes total frying time per slice.
8. Remove the slices to a baking sheet lined with paper towels.
9. Continue until all the pickle slices are fried.
10. Serve with sauce for dipping.

VIDEO: Frying pickles

Creamy Cucumber and Sweet Onion Salad

serves 6 to 8

20 minutes till it's ready, plus chill time

- 4 large cucumbers, halved lengthwise, seeded, and sliced into ¼-inch slices, about 4 cups
- 1 teaspoon kosher salt
- 1 medium white onion, peeled and thinly sliced, about 1 cup
- 1 cup mayonnaise
- 1 cup sour cream
- ⅓ cup white wine vinegar
- 2 tablespoons granulated sugar
- 2 tablespoons chopped fresh dill

1. Dump the cucumber slices into a colander in the sink.
2. Lightly sprinkle the cucumber with salt. Let sit for 15 to 20 minutes so that the excess moisture is released.
3. Rinse with cold water and pat dry.
4. Place the cucumbers and sliced onion into a bowl.
5. Whisk together the mayonnaise, sour cream, vinegar, and sugar in a small bowl. Pour this mixture over the cucumbers and onions. Toss and then chill in the fridge for at least 30 minutes.
6. Sprinkle with fresh dill.

Eggplant is the perfect veggie for meatless main dishes because of its dense texture. My favorite eggplant recipes are the ones where eggplant is the star of the casserole, like this one for the iconic eggplant and spicy lamb combination topped with a decadent béchamel sauce.

For eggplant:
- 3 large eggplants, peeled and sliced into ½-inch thick lengths
- 1 teaspoon kosher salt
- 1 teaspoon coarse black pepper
- ½ cup olive oil
- 2 large garlic cloves, minced, about 1 tablespoon
- 1 teaspoon dried oregano
- 1 teaspoon dried cumin

For lamb ragù:
- 2 tablespoons olive oil
- 1 large yellow onion, diced into ½-inch squares, about 1 ½ cup
- 2 large carrots, peeled and diced, about 1 cup
- 2 garlic cloves, minced, about 1 tablespoon

1. Preheat your oven to 425°.
2. Season the eggplants with salt and freshly ground pepper.
3. Place in a colander for 30 minutes to draw out excess moisture.
4. Stir together ½ cup olive oil and the garlic, oregano, and cumin.
5. Brush both sides of the eggplant with the seasoned olive oil.
6. Arrange slices onto a baking sheet. (They can overlap.) Roast until the slices are tender and golden, about 30 minutes.
7. Reduce the oven temperature to 350°.
8. Heat 2 more tablespoons of olive oil in a skillet over medium-high heat.
9. Cook the onion and carrots until soft and golden, about 5 to 7 minutes.
10. Add the garlic and cook for 2 minutes more.
11. Add the lamb to the skillet. Cook, breaking up the meat with a spatula, until browned, about 8 to 10 minutes.

Eggplant

Moussaka Casserole
serves 6 to 8
1 hour till it's done

- 2 pounds lean ground lamb
- 1 cup red wine
- 1 (16-ounce) can diced tomatoes
- 2 tablespoons tomato paste
- 1 teaspoon dried oregano
- 1 cinnamon stick

For béchamel topping:
- 3 tablespoons butter
- 3 tablespoons all-purpose flour
- 2 cups milk
- 1 cup ricotta cheese
- 4 ounces finely grated Parmesan cheese, about ½ cup
- ½ teaspoon ground nutmeg
- 2 tablespoons chopped fresh mint

12. Stir in the wine, tomatoes, tomato paste, oregano, and cinnamon stick. Reduce the heat to medium and simmer the ragù for 15 minutes. Season with salt and pepper. Remove the cinnamon stick.
13. Heat the butter in a deep pot over medium-high heat. Whisk in the flour. Cook until golden and bubbling, about 2 to 4 minutes.
14. Pour in the milk. Cook, stirring constantly, until the sauce is thickened, about 6 to 8 minutes.
15. Stir in the ricotta and Parmesan cheeses. Season with ground nutmeg, salt, and pepper.
16. Assemble the casserole by placing a layer of eggplant slices in the bottom of a 13 x 9 x 2-inch baking dish. Top with half of lamb ragù. Add another layer of eggplant and another layer of lamb. Finish with a layer of eggplant.
17. Top the casserole with béchamel sauce.
18. Bake until the casserole is bubbly and the top is golden, about 30 to 40 minutes.
19. Allow the casserole to sit for 15 minutes before serving. Garnish with fresh mint.

Eggplant Parmesan

serves 8

30 minutes till it's ready

- 1 large eggplant, cut into ¾-inch slices
- 1 teaspoon kosher salt
- 1 teaspoon coarse black pepper
- 1 cup unbleached all-purpose flour
- 2 large eggs, beaten

- 2 cups seasoned panko breadcrumbs
- vegetable oil for frying
- 2 cups marinara sauce
- 16 ounces fresh mozzarella cheese, thinly sliced
- 4 ounces Parmesan cheese, grated, about 1 cup

1. Preheat your oven to 375°.
2. Season the eggplant with salt and pepper.
3. Dredge a slice of eggplant first in the flour, then through the beaten egg (shaking off the excess), and finally into the breadcrumbs.
4. Lay the coated eggplant onto a baking rack or piece of parchment paper and continue with the remaining slices.
5. Heat about an inch of vegetable oil in a cast iron skillet over medium-high heat. Carefully drop some of the eggplant slices into the hot oil. Don't overcrowd the pan.
6. Cook until the eggplant is golden on one side, about 3 to 4 minutes. Carefully turn the eggplant and cook until golden on the second side, about 3 minutes more.
7. Transfer the eggplant slices to a paper-towel lined platter.
8. Pour enough marinara sauce into a baking dish to coat the bottom. Lay the eggplant slices into the dish. Top with the remaining marinara sauce. Distribute the mozzarella cheese over the top of the eggplant and sprinkle Parmesan over everything.
9. Bake until the cheese is melted and gooey, about 20 minutes.

When I'm shopping the market, I always buy plenty of greens. I just love the bunches of tender leaves and everything you can do with them. Different greens will cook in different lengths of time. The more tender the green, the faster it will wilt in the pan—like spinach. The denser the leaf, like collards or mustard greens or Swiss chard, the longer they will take to prepare.

You can use the essence of the greens to flavor oils and sauces. You can also add greens to your favorite casseroles, mound them on pizza, or like the next recipe, combine greens into one super-satisfying frittata.

Greens

Ricotta Frittata
with Swiss Chard and Spinach
serves 6 to 8
45 minutes till it's ready

- 1 tablespoon olive oil
- ¾ pound mild Italian pork sausage
- 1 bunch green onions, thinly sliced, about 1 cup
- 1 bunch Swiss chard, chopped, about 3 to 4 cups
- ½ pound fresh spinach leaves, chopped, about 3 to 4 cups
- 1 teaspoon kosher salt
- 1 teaspoon coarse black pepper

- ½ teaspoon ground nutmeg
- 12 large eggs
- 4 ounces Gruyère cheese, grated, about ½ cup, divided
- 2 cups crushed salt and vinegar potato chips
- 4 ounces ricotta cheese, about 1 cup
- roasted cherry tomatoes
- chopped fresh parsley

1. Preheat the oven to 350°.
2. Heat the olive oil in a 12-inch oven-safe skillet over medium-high heat. Add the sausage and cook until browned and crumbly, about 5 to 8 minutes. Transfer the sausage to a bowl. Drain all but about 1 tablespoon of the drippings from the pan.
3. Add the onions to the pan and cook until soft, about 5 minutes. Add the Swiss chard and cook until wilted, about 2 minutes.
4. Add the spinach and cook until wilted, about 2 minutes more.
5. Season with salt, pepper, and nutmeg.
6. Reduce the heat to medium.
7. Crack the eggs into a large bowl. Whisk in half of the grated cheese and all the potato chips. Stir in the ricotta cheese.

8. Transfer the sausage back into the skillet.
9. Pour the egg and cheese mixture into the skillet, spreading evenly.
10. Cook on stovetop until the frittata is set on the edges but the center still wiggles, about 10 minutes. Sprinkle the top with the remaining grated cheese.
11. Place the skillet into the oven and bake until the center is set, about 20 minutes. Use a sharp knife to loosen the edges of the frittata. Serve the frittata from the skillet or use a spatula to gently slide the frittata onto a serving platter.
12. Garnish with fresh parsley and roasted cherry tomatoes.

Sautéed Collard Greens
with Fresh Ginger
serves a crowd
about an hour till it's done

- 2 ounces bacon, diced, about 4 slices
- 1 (3-inch) piece fresh ginger, peeled and finely diced, about 3 tablespoons
- ½ medium red onion, peeled and diced, about ½ cup
- 1 small bell pepper, deveined and diced, about ½ cup
- 1 teaspoon ground coriander
- 1 teaspoon ground paprika
- 1 teaspoon ground cumin
- 1 teaspoon kosher salt
- ½ teaspoon coarse black pepper
- 1 pound collard greens, stems removed, leaves rolled, thinly sliced and then cut in half crosswise, about 8 cups
- 2 cups chicken stock
- ¼ cup soy sauce
- 1 tablespoon honey

1. Place the bacon into a sauté pan with lid over medium heat. Cook until the bacon renders fat and just begins to crisp, about 2 minutes.
2. Add the ginger, onion, and bell pepper. Cook until the veggies are soft, about 2 minutes more.
3. Season with coriander, paprika, cumin, salt, and pepper.
4. Add the collard greens. Toss to coat the greens with the spices and veggies.
5. Pour in one cup of stock, then the soy sauce and honey.
6. Cover and simmer over low heat for 20 minutes.
7. Remove the lid and pour in the rest of the chicken stock and continue simmering until the collards are very soft, about 30 minutes more.
8. Taste and season with more salt and pepper.

Thing to Note:
If you find young, fresh ginger that doesn't need peeling, this is the time to use it! The flavor is not as strong, but it's just as good.

VIDEO: Peeling and mincing ginger

Mince Ginger

VIDEO: Rolling and chopping collard greens

Collard Greens

Spinach au Gratin

with Sautéed Mushrooms
serves 4 to 6
30 minutes till it's ready

For mushrooms:
- 2 tablespoons olive oil
- 2 tablespoons butter
- 12 ounces mushrooms, you choose the type, sliced or chopped, about 2 cups
- ¼ cup sherry
- 1 teaspoon kosher salt
- ½ teaspoon coarse black pepper

For spinach:
- 1 (20-ounce) package frozen chopped spinach, thawed and drained (you can substitute with fresh spinach leaves)
- 3 tablespoons butter, divided
- 2 tablespoons unbleached all-purpose flour
- 1 ½ cups milk
- ¼ teaspoon nutmeg
- 4 ounces Gruyère cheese, grated, about ½ cup
- 2 ounces Parmesan cheese, grated, about ¼ cup
- paprika

1. Heat the olive oil and 2 tablespoons butter in a pot over medium-high heat.
2. Add the mushrooms. Don't mess with them! Let the mushrooms cook until they are golden brown on the bottom, about 4 to 5 minutes. Turn them to cook on the second side, about 2 more minutes.
3. Reduce the heat to medium and pour in the sherry. Cook until the liquid disappears, about 3 minutes more.
4. Season with some of the salt and pepper. Turn off the heat.
5. Preheat your oven to 375°.
6. Cook the spinach in the microwave. Drain in a colander and use paper towels to press out excess moisture.
7. Heat 2 tablespoons of butter in a pot over medium heat until melted.
8. Stir in the flour and cook until the mixture begins to bubble.
9. Pour in the milk and stir until the sauce begins to thicken, about 5 minutes. Season with salt, pepper, and nutmeg.
10. Remove the pot from the heat and stir in the Gruyère cheese until melted.
11. Place the spinach into a bowl. Pour in half of the sauce and stir. Pour in the remaining sauce and stir once more.
12. Pour the spinach mixture into a casserole dish (or several smaller individual casserole dishes).
13. Top the spinach mixture with the mushrooms and sprinkle with Parmesan cheese. Cut the remaining one tablespoon of butter into tiny pieces and dot the top of the casserole, then sprinkle with a bit of paprika.
14. Cook until the top is golden and the casserole is bubbling, about 20 to 30 minutes.

Things to Note:
If you choose to use fresh spinach, 1 pound of fresh spinach will cook down to about the same amount as 10 ounces of cooked frozen spinach. For this recipe, you will need 2 pounds of fresh spinach, chopped, which will be about 8 cups. Steam the spinach in a microwave oven or in a steamer over boiling water. Drain as directed above.

Mushrooms

Mushrooms are great. Another meaty veggie, perfect for entrees, the versatile 'shroom will absorb all of the flavors you can throw at it!

Roasted Wild Mushroom Soup
serves 4
30 minutes till it's ready

- ¾ pound assorted wild mushrooms
- 2 tablespoons olive oil
- 1 teaspoon coarse black pepper
- 4 cups chicken stock
- 2 tablespoons butter
- 1 medium shallot, peeled and finely diced, about ¼ cup
- 1 tablespoon chopped fresh thyme leaves
- 1 teaspoon kosher salt
- 1 cup brandy (You don't have to use the good stuff!)
- 2 tablespoons unbleached, all-purpose flour
- 1 cup heavy cream

1. Preheat your oven to 425°.
2. Spread the mushrooms onto a baking sheet. If there are larger 'shrooms, you can tear them into smaller pieces. To cook equally, you want similar-sized pieces.
3. Drizzle with olive oil and season with pepper.

4. Roast the mushrooms until the edges are beginning to crisp and they are reduced in size, about 10 to 15 minutes.
5. Transfer most of the mushrooms to a blender. Keep a couple of pieces for garnish! Cover with some of the stock, about 1 to 2 cups. Pulse to create a smooth puree. If you need more stock, go ahead and add it here.
6. Heat the butter in a deep pot over medium heat.
7. Add the shallot and cook until softened, about 3 to 4 minutes.
8. Add the thyme and season with salt.
9. Pour in the brandy. Bring to a boil and reduce the heat to simmer. When the brandy is reduced to almost no liquid, add the flour and stir.
10. Add the mushroom puree and remaining stock. Simmer until the soup begins to thicken.
11. Stir in the cream.
12. Taste and season with more salt.
13. Pour the soup into bowls and top with a bit of thyme and mushroom pieces.

Thing to Note:
When you season with salt, you draw out the moisture in a thing (think cabbage, eggplant, and beef). We want the moisture to stay in these mushrooms while they are roasting. That's why you season with pepper before and add a bit of salt afterward.

Veggie Enchiladas
with Grilled Portobello Mushrooms, Corn, and Black Beans
serves 4 to 6
40 minutes till it's ready

For sauce:
- 3 tablespoons chili powder
- 3 tablespoons unbleached all-purpose flour
- 1 teaspoon cocoa powder
- ½ teaspoon garlic powder
- 1 teaspoon dried oregano
- 1 tablespoon tomato paste
- 1 (15.5 ounce) can crushed tomatoes

For enchiladas:
- 4 portobello mushroom caps, stems and gills removed
- 4 tablespoons olive oil, divided
- 1 teaspoon kosher salt
- ½ teaspoon coarse black pepper
- 1 medium red onion, peeled and finely diced, about 1 cup
- 1 large red bell pepper, seeded, veins removed, and diced, about 1 cup
- 1 (10-ounce) package frozen white corn, thawed
- 1 (15.5-ounce) can black beans, drained and rinsed
- 1 teaspoon chili powder
- 4 (8-inch diameter) flour tortillas
- 8 ounces sharp cheddar cheese, grated, about 2 cups (reserve some for garnish)
- 4 to 5 green onions, thinly sliced, about ½ cup

1. Make the enchilada sauce by whisking together chili powder, flour, cocoa powder, garlic powder, and oregano in a small pot.
2. Whisk in about ½ cup of water to create a smooth paste.
3. Warm the paste over medium-high heat for about 1 minute.
4. Whisk in tomato paste and another 2 to 2 ½ cups water and bring to a boil.
5. Reduce the heat to medium-low and simmer, whisking constantly, until the sauce begins to thicken.
6. Whisk in crushed tomatoes.
7. Set the sauce aside while you continue the recipe.
8. Spray a grill pan with vegetable oil spray.
9. Heat the grill to medium-high.
10. Drizzle the mushrooms with 2 tablespoons olive oil and place into the pan, cap side down. Grill the mushrooms, turning once, until just beginning to soften. Season with salt and pepper. Remove to a platter and cool slightly.
11. Cut the mushrooms into ½-inch slices.
12. Heat the remaining 2 tablespoons olive oil in a skillet over medium heat. Cook the onion, pepper, corn, and black beans in the skillet until the vegetables are soft. Season with chili powder, salt, and pepper.
13. Preheat your oven to 350°.
14. Pour some of the enchilada sauce in the bottom of a baking dish. Lay one flour tortilla onto your work surface. Spread the tortilla with cheese. Top with a layer of sautéed veggies. Lay slices of grilled mushroom over the top. Roll the tortilla around the veggies.
15. Lay the enchilada in the baking dish and continue with remaining ingredients. Cover the enchiladas with the remaining sauce and sprinkle extra cheese on the top.
16. Bake the enchiladas in the oven until the cheese is melted and the sauce bubbles, about 15 to 20 minutes. Garnish with green onions.

Peppers

Mexican-Style Stuffed Bell Peppers
serves 4
45 minutes till it's ready

- 4 large bell peppers, sliced in half, stem tops, seeds, and veins removed, making 8 pepper "cups"
- 1 tablespoon olive oil, plus 2 more for filling
- 1 teaspoon kosher salt
- 1 teaspoon coarse black pepper
- 1 medium onion, cut into ¼-inch pieces, about 1 cup
- 1 medium zucchini, cut into ¼-inch pieces, about 1 cup
- 2 ears of corn, kernels removed, about 1 cup
- 1 (15-ounce) can black beans, drained and rinsed
- 1 small jalapeño pepper, seeded, veins removed, diced, about 2 tablespoons
- 1 (14-ounce) jar prepared enchilada sauce
- 2 tablespoons chopped fresh cilantro
- 4 ounces Monterey Jack cheese, shredded, about 1 cup
- 1 cup tortilla chips, crushed

Thing to Note:
These peppers are terrific for the veggie conscious ... but you can beef them up for the Meat Lover in your family. Just change up the filling. It's all good!

Since we're taking a little veggie trip south of the border, why not take a look at this recipe featuring bell peppers?

1. Preheat your oven to 375°.
2. Add the peppers to a baking dish, cut sides up. Drizzle the insides of the peppers with 1 tablespoon olive oil and some of the salt and pepper. Place into the oven and bake to soften, about 5 minutes. Remove to cool slightly.
3. Drizzle 2 tablespoons olive oil in a large skillet over medium-high heat. Add the onion and zucchini and cook until the veggies are softened, about 5 to 8 minutes.
4. Stir in the corn, black beans, and jalapeño pepper. Cook for several minutes more.
5. Pour in the enchilada sauce. Stir in the cilantro. Reduce the heat to low and simmer until the veggies are soft and the sauce is reduced by half. You want a thick stew of veggies, not a soupy sauce. Taste and season with salt.
6. Fill half of each pepper with veggies.
7. Add some of the cheese and top that with some of the chips. Place the remaining veggies over the chips. Top with the rest of the cheese and the chips.
8. Place the baking dish back into the oven and cook until the cheese is melted and the chips are golden, about 15 minutes.

VIDEO: Stuffing peppers

Roasted Peppers
stuffed with Tuna and Olive Salad
serves 6
30 minutes till it's ready

For peppers:
- 3 large yellow or red bell peppers
- 1 (8-ounce) tuna steak
- 1 tablespoon olive oil
- 1 teaspoon kosher salt
- ½ teaspoon coarse black pepper
- 2 large eggs, hard boiled, peeled, and sliced
- 10 to 12 Niçoise (or other good quality) olives, pitted
- 4 to 6 (2-inch) red potatoes, boiled until tender, cut in half
- 8 ounces petite green beans, blanched, chopped into 1-inch pieces
- 1 (2-ounce) tin anchovies, packed in oil, drained, and chopped

For dressing:
- 1 tablespoon Dijon mustard
- 1 tablespoon chopped fresh tarragon
- 1 medium garlic clove, minced, about ½ teaspoon
- juice of 1 lemon, about 2 tablespoons
- ⅓ cup tarragon vinegar
- ¾ cup olive oil

1. Char the outside of the peppers over a hot grill or flame, or underneath the broiler in the oven. The peppers should be black on all sides.
2. Place the peppers into a paper bag or a bowl covered with plastic to steam for at least 15 minutes.
3. Brush the tuna steak with 1 tablespoon olive oil. Season with some of the salt and pepper.
4. Grill over a hot flame until just rare on the inside, about 4 minutes per side for a 1-inch thick steak. Cut the tuna into bite-size pieces and place into a bowl.
5. Add the sliced egg, olives, potatoes, green beans, and anchovies. Toss with fresh pepper.
6. Whisk together the mustard, tarragon, garlic, lemon juice, and vinegar. Slowly whisk in ¾ cup olive oil.
7. Peel the charred skin from the peppers. Cut each one in half. Remove the seeds.
8. Place a pepper half on a plate. Place a spoonful of the tuna mixture into each half. Drizzle the dressing over the tuna salad and the pepper.

VIDEO: Roasting peppers

Potatoes

You say potato and I say ... give me more! I love all sorts of potato treatments—mashed, fried, roasted, hashed, baked, and baked again. Are you getting a hint at my devotion? Once you have mastered all these common preparations, try one of these recipes to take your spud addiction to the next level.

Mashed Potato Croquettes
yields about a dozen 3-inch croquettes
30 minutes till they're ready

- 4 cups leftover mashed potatoes
- 2 eggs, (separate 1 egg into yolk and white)
- 3 tablespoons milk
- 2 green onions, thinly sliced, about 2 tablespoons
- 1 teaspoon kosher salt
- 1 teaspoon coarse black pepper
- 2 cups seasoned breadcrumbs
- canola (or vegetable) oil for frying
- sea salt
- chopped fresh herbs

1. Place the mashed potatoes in a bowl. Stir in 1 egg yolk, milk, and green onions. Season with salt and pepper.
2. Place the bowl into the fridge for a couple of minutes while you assemble the breading station.
3. Crack 1 whole egg and add the reserved egg white to a shallow bowl. Add 1 to 2 tablespoons of water and whisk to combine.
4. Place the seasoned breadcrumbs in another shallow bowl.
5. Remove the potatoes from the fridge. Use an ice cream scoop to form round potato balls. Dip a ball first into the egg wash and then into the breadcrumbs.
6. Transfer each ball to a parchment-lined sheet pan or platter. When all the croquettes are formed, place them back into the fridge for 15 minutes.
7. Heat oil in a fryer or deep pot to 375°. (You can use a candy thermometer to measure the temperature.)
8. Fry the croquettes in the oil a couple at a time until deeply golden. Transfer to a paper-towel lined platter. When all the croquettes are fried, garnish with a touch of sea salt and fresh herbs.

Make Ahead Tip:
You can make these ahead of time and store in an airtight container in the fridge. Bring them to room temperature before you fry.

Pommes de Terre Chantilly

serves 4

30 minutes till they're ready

- 3 large (about 9 ounces each) baking potatoes, peeled and cut into ½-inch pieces, about 6 cups
- 3 tablespoons butter, room temperature, plus 1 tablespoon for baking dish
- 1 tablespoon kosher salt
- ⅓ cup milk
- ¾ cup heavy whipping cream, chilled
- 1 ounce Parmesan cheese, grated, about ¼ cup

1. Add the potatoes to a pot with salted boiling water. Cook until the potatoes are very soft, about 8 to 10 minutes. Use a colander to drain the potatoes.
2. Place 3 tablespoons room-temperature butter and the milk into a large bowl. Use a potato ricer to mash up the potatoes. Stir into a smooth puree.
3. Preheat your oven to 400°.
4. Use an electric mixer to whip the cream into soft peaks.
5. Place about ⅓ of the whipped cream into the center of the potatoes. Gently stir the cream into the potatoes. The potatoes will be soft and light.
6. Scrape the remaining whipped cream into the bowl with the potatoes. Gently fold this cream into the potatoes. You don't need to overwork the potatoes. You want these to be light and airy.
7. Divide 1 tablespoon butter into four individual baking dishes. Place these into a larger baking dish. Place in the oven and let the butter melt on the bottom of each one, about 2 to 3 minutes. (If you don't want to serve in individual containers, simply melt the butter in one large baking dish.)
8. Remove the hot dishes (use a potholder).
9. Spoon in the potatoes. Sprinkle each dish with Parmesan cheese. Bake until the potatoes are warmed through and the tops begin to turn golden brown on the edges, about 20 to 25 minutes.

VIDEO: Ricing potatoes

Here's another outstanding potato dish. Leftover baked potatoes will give you a running start because they need to be cold to get the proper texture. It's well worth the extra step!

Make Ahead Tip:
You can substitute black pepper for white. No problem. And the sharper the cheese you pick, the better the dish, so pick one you would be happy eating on a cracker.

Potatoes Romanoff
serves 6 to 8
75 minutes till it's ready, plus some chill time
(at least six hours or overnight)

- 3 large baking potatoes
- 2 tablespoons olive oil
- 1 tablespoon kosher salt
- 2 large shallots, peeled and minced
- 1 teaspoon ground white pepper
- 8 ounces white cheddar cheese, grated, about 2 cups
- 2 cups sour cream
- 2 tablespoons butter, cut into very small pieces

1. Preheat your oven to 400°.
2. Pierce the potatoes with the tines of a fork. Add them to a baking dish.
3. Roll the potatoes in olive oil and sprinkle with some of the salt.
4. Bake until the potatoes are cooked through, about 45 minutes to 1 hour. Cool the potatoes to room temperature.
5. Wrap each in plastic wrap and refrigerate for at least 6 hours or overnight. The potatoes need to be very cold to shred well.
6. Preheat your oven to 425°.
7. Use a box grater to shred the potatoes into a large bowl.
8. Add the shallots and season with salt and white pepper.
9. Use two forks to gently mix everything together. You want the mixture to be light and fluffy, so don't overmix.
10. Add the cheese and mix again (using those two forks). Add the sour cream and mix until just combined.
11. Pile the potatoes into a baking dish that has been coated with vegetable oil spray.
12. Dot the top of the potatoes with bits of butter.
13. Bake the potatoes until top is just turning golden brown, about 30 to 35 minutes.

Squish, squash! What a wonderful mash-up of a terrific veggie and so many preparations. Everything from zucchini casseroles to pumpkin pies start with one great squash! Here are a couple of my favorite squash recipes.

Squash

Risotto with Butternut Squash

serves 4
20 minutes till it's ready

- 1 tablespoon olive oil
- ½ red onion, peeled and diced, about ½ cup
- ½ medium butternut squash, peeled and diced into small chunks, about 2 cups
- 1 teaspoon chili powder
- 1 teaspoon garlic powder
- 1 teaspoon onion powder
- ½ teaspoon ground cumin
- ½ teaspoon ground cinnamon
- 1 teaspoon kosher salt
- ½ teaspoon coarse black pepper
- 1 cup Arborio rice
- ¼ cup dry sherry
- 3 to 4 cups chicken stock, warmed in a pot over low heat
- ¼ cup heavy cream
- 1 tablespoon butter
- 2 ounces Parmesan cheese, grated
- 2 tablespoons chopped fresh parsley

1. Heat olive oil in a skillet over medium-high heat.
2. Add the onion and cook until soft, about 3 minutes.
3. Add the butternut squash. Sprinkle with the seasonings, salt, and pepper and cook for 3 minutes more.
4. Add the rice and cook for 1 more minute to toast.
5. Pour in the sherry and cook until the liquid disappears, about 2 minutes.
6. Reduce the heat to medium-low.
7. Pour in about 1 cup of the chicken stock. Bring to a simmer and cook until the liquid disappears, about 5 minutes.
8. Add 1 more cup chicken stock. Continue, using all of the stock until the rice absorbs all the liquid.
9. The rice should be creamy with just an itty bit of crunch. You don't want it to be too mushy!
10. Stir in the cream, butter, and Parmesan cheese. Sprinkle with parsley.

Pumpkin Hummus
with Homemade Pita wedges and Crudité
serves a crowd
30 minutes till it's ready

For Hummus:
- 1 (15-ounce) can chickpeas, drained and rinsed
- 1 cup pumpkin puree
- ¼ cup olive oil
- 4 garlic cloves, peeled
- juice of ½ medium lemon, about 1 tablespoon
- 1 tablespoon chopped fresh thyme
- 1 teaspoon paprika
- 1 teaspoon kosher salt
- 1 teaspoon coarse black pepper

For Pita Chips:
- 4 whole pitas, cut into wedges (about 32 total)
- 4 tablespoons butter, melted
- 2 ounces Parmesan cheese, grated, about ½ cup

For Crudité:
- celery sticks
- carrot sticks
- radishes, sliced
- petite green beans
- bell peppers, sliced into strips

1. Add the chickpeas, pumpkin puree, olive oil, garlic, lemon juice, thyme, and paprika to the bowl of a food processor. Pulse to form a smooth paste. Season with salt and pepper.
2. Pour the pumpkin hummus into a bowl.
3. Preheat your oven to 375°.
4. Place the pita wedges onto a baking sheet.
5. Brush with butter and sprinkle with Parmesan cheese.
6. Bake until the tops of the pitas are golden, about 5 to 7 minutes.
7. Serve the hummus with warm pita wedges and crudité.

VIDEO: Making hummus

Butternut Squash Bisque

serves 6 to 8

40 minutes till it's ready

- ¼ cup olive oil
- 4 tablespoons butter, ½ stick
- 1 leek, sliced in half, rinsed, white and tender green parts sliced, about 1 cup
- 1 yellow onion, peeled and chopped, about 1 cup
- 1 (2 pound) butternut squash, peeled and chopped, about 5 to 6 cups
- 4 whole garlic cloves, peeled, about 2 tablespoons
- 1 tablespoon pumpkin pie spice
- 1 tablespoon chili powder
- 1 teaspoon kosher salt
- ½ teaspoon coarse black pepper
- ⅓ cup sherry
- 1 quart chicken stock
- ¾ cup heavy whipping cream

1. Heat the olive oil and butter in a large pot over medium-high heat.
2. Add the leek and onion to the pan and cook until the veggies are soft, about 5 to 7 minutes.
3. Add butternut squash and garlic. Season with spice blend, chili powder, salt, and pepper.
4. Pour in the sherry and cook until most of the liquid is absorbed into the veggies.
5. Pour in the stock.
6. Reduce the heat to medium-low and simmer until all the veggies are very soft, about 20 minutes.
7. Remove the pot from the heat.
8. Use an immersion blender, food processor, or blender to emulsify the soup. If you are using a blender or food processor, allow the soup to cool before pulsing ... just to be safe!
9. Return the pureed soup to the pot over low heat. Stir in the cream.
10. Taste and season with salt and pepper.

Zucchini
topped with Roasted Tomatoes and Pine Nuts
serves 4 to 6
30 minutes till it's ready

- 2 pints grape tomatoes, halved, about 4 cups
- 8 large garlic cloves, peeled and thinly sliced, about ¼ cup
- fresh thyme sprigs
- 1 teaspoon granulated sugar
- 1 teaspoon kosher salt
- ½ teaspoon coarse black pepper
- 2 tablespoons olive oil, plus 2 more for zucchini
- ⅓ cup kalamata olives, pitted and chopped
- 2 tablespoons capers, rinsed
- 2 large zucchinis, cut into 1-inch rounds, about 4 cups
- ¼ cup water
- ⅛ teaspoon baking soda
- 1 (2-ounce) package pine nuts, toasted, about ½ cup
- zest of 1 medium lemon, about 2 tablespoons

1. Preheat to oven to 350°.
2. Add the tomatoes to a baking sheet. Toss the garlic and thyme sprigs around the tomatoes.
3. Drizzle with sugar, salt, pepper, and 2 tablespoons olive oil. Toss gently.
4. Roast until the tomatoes begin to burst and the garlic is soft and golden, about 20 minutes.
5. Remove from the oven and toss with the olives and capers. Set aside.
6. Heat the remaining 2 tablespoons olive oil in a skillet over medium heat.
7. Place the zucchini into the skillet in a single layer. Season with salt.
8. Add ¼ cup water and a pinch of baking soda.
9. Cook, turning often, until the water evaporates and the zucchini is just soft and golden, about 15 to 20 minutes. Be patient; this step is worth the effort. The zucchini will look like little pillows!
10. Transfer the zucchini to a baking dish. Cover each piece with a spoonful of the tomato mixture. Sprinkle with pine nuts.
11. Bake until the dish is warmed through, about 10 minutes.
12. Grate the lemon zest overtop and serve warm.

Roasted Zucchini Blossoms

serves 4 to 6

30 minutes till it's ready

- 1 tablespoon butter
- 4 ounces mushrooms, finely diced, about 1 cup
- 1 teaspoon kosher salt
- 1 teaspoon coarse black pepper
- 1 tablespoon chopped fresh thyme
- 4 slices bacon, cooked and finely diced
- 1 cup ricotta cheese
- 2 tablespoons Parmesan cheese
- 1 egg yolk
- 2 tablespoons olive oil, divided
- 12 to 14 zucchini blossoms

1. Preheat the oven to 375°.
2. Heat the butter over medium-high heat.
3. Add the mushrooms. Season with some salt and pepper. Sprinkle with thyme. Cook until golden, about 2 to 3 minutes.
4. Place the bacon into a bowl. Add the ricotta, Parmesan, and egg yolk and stir. Fold in the mushrooms. Season with salt and pepper.
5. Drizzle a baking sheet with 1 tablespoon olive oil.
6. Gently open the petals of one blossom. Use a spoon (or pastry bag) to place some of the filling into the center of the blossom. Close the petals over the filling and place onto the baking sheet. Repeat with the remaining blossoms. Drizzle with olive oil.
7. Bake until the filling is melted and warmed through, about 8 to 10 minutes. Serve warm.

Make Ahead Tip:

If you have extra filling, you can use it to make cheesy ravioli. Use wonton wrappers as the base. Place one wrap onto your work surface. Use a pastry brush to moisten the outer edges of the wrap. Place a spoonful of filling in the center and top with a second wrapper. Use the tines of a fork to close the wrapper. Drop them into boiling water for a minute or two, and you have yummy, cheesy ravioli.

VIDEO: Roasting Blossoms

Tomatoes

My absolute favorite veggie is the tomato ... which is really a fruit, but who's counting? I love the ones you find in the middle of the summer that are deep purply-red with evergreen stripes. These are the sweetest of all the varieties. However, all it takes is a sprinkle of salt and a dash of sugar to make that winter tomato taste just as yummy. Here are a couple of my favorite tomato recipes.

Thing to Note:
To peel the tomatoes and peaches, use a sharp knife to cut slits in the top. Place into boiling water for a minute or two. Remove and cool slightly. The peel will come off easily from the slits.

VIDEO: Making chutney

Chutney

Tomato and Peach Chutney
makes about 3 cups
30 minutes till it's ready

- 1 tablespoon olive oil
- 1 poblano pepper, seeded and finely diced, about ½ cup
- 2 to 3 medium-hot cherry peppers, seeded and finely diced, about ½ cup
- ½ medium red onion, peeled and finely diced, about ½ cup
- 6 medium tomatoes, peeled and diced, about 6 cups
- 6 ripe peaches, peeled and diced, about 6 cups
- 2 tablespoons brown sugar
- 1 teaspoon Chinese five spice
- 1 teaspoon kosher salt
- ½ teaspoon coarse black pepper

1. Heat the olive oil in a large pot over medium-high heat.
2. Add the peppers and onion and cook until just soft, about 2 to 3 minutes.
3. Stir in the tomatoes and peaches.
4. Stir in the brown sugar.
5. Bring everything to a boil and then reduce the heat to medium-low.
6. Season with Chinese five spice, salt, and pepper.
7. Simmer until the peaches just begin to break apart and the chutney thickens, about 20 to 25 minutes. The longer you simmer, the thicker the chutney!
8. Cool to room temperature and the store in an airtight container for up to 3 weeks in the fridge.

To get a running start with this recipe, you can purchase a frozen pie crust and then partially bake it before you fill it with tomatoey goodness. You can also make a pie crust and parbake it using pie weights.

Tomato Pie
serves 6 to 8
40 minutes till it's ready

- 4 large tomatoes
- 1 teaspoon kosher salt
- 4 ounces mozzarella cheese, grated, about 1 cup
- 4 ounces cheddar cheese, grated, about 1 cup
- 1 cup mayonnaise
- 1 bunch green onions, thinly sliced
- ½ teaspoon black pepper
- 4 to 6 slices bacon, cooked and crumbled
- 1 parbaked pie shell
- 3 tablespoons chopped fresh basil
- assorted microgreens for garnish

1. Preheat your oven to 350°.
2. Slice the tomatoes and place them into a colander. Sprinkle the tomatoes with salt and let them sit for 10 minutes to release some of their juices.
3. Mix the cheeses and mayonnaise. Stir in the green onions. Season with salt and pepper.
4. Sprinkle the bacon over the bottom of the pie crust.
5. Layer the tomatoes on top of the bacon. Sprinkle the tomatoes with basil.
6. Spoon cheese topping over everything.
7. Bake the pie until the topping begins to turn golden and is melty and bubbling, about 15 to 20 minutes.
8. Remove the pie from the oven and cool.
9. Spread the microgreens over the top of the pie. Serve warm or at room temperature.

Thing to Note:
You get a head start on this delicious dish by using a refrigerated pie crust. We want to partially bake the crust before we fill it and then bake it again with the cheesy filling inside. To parbake the crust, preheat your oven to 400°. Lay the pie dough into a pie pan and crinkle the edges. Pierce the bottom of the dough with the tines of a fork. Lay a piece of parchment paper over the pie shell. Fill with pie weights or dried beans. Bake until the edges begin to turn golden, about 10 to 15 minutes. Remove the pie shell from the oven. Remove the parchment paper and the weights. Now you are ready to go! Layer the pie shell with all of your yummy tomato pie ingredients and finish in the oven.

VIDEO: Parbaking pie crust

Tomato Soup
with Jalapeño and a Hint of Fennel
serves 4 to 6
40 minutes till it's ready

- 2 tablespoons olive oil
- 1 medium red onion, diced into small cubes, about 1 cup
- 1 small jalapeño pepper, seeded and diced, about 2 tablespoons
- 4 garlic cloves, peeled and crushed, about 2 tablespoons
- 1 teaspoon dried basil
- ½ cup dry sherry
- 1 (28-ounce) can crushed tomatoes
- 4 ounces tomato paste, about ½ cup
- 1 quart chicken stock
- 1 teaspoon kosher salt
- 1 teaspoon coarse black pepper
- 1 teaspoon granulated sugar
- ½ large fennel bulb, leaves trimmed and cut in half
- ½ cup half-and-half
- ¼ cup sour cream

1. Pour olive oil into the bottom of a large pot over medium-high heat.
2. Place the onion and pepper into the pot and cook until soft and fragrant, about 2 to 3 minutes.
3. Stir in the garlic and basil and cook for 1 minute more.
4. Pour in the sherry and simmer until most of the liquid disappears, about 3 to 5 minutes.
5. Pour in the tomatoes, tomato paste, and chicken stock. Season with salt, pepper, and sugar.
6. Drop the fennel bulb into the soup.
7. Reduce the heat to low, cover the pot with a lid, and simmer the soup for 20 minutes, allowing the flavors to blend.
8. Remove the pot from the heat.
9. Remove and discard the fennel bulb.
10. Stir in the half-and-half and sour cream.
11. Serve the soup with crushed crackers, another dollop of sour cream, and the leafy tops from the fennel.

All Things Food

Now that we've covered all things veggie, look out for Volume 3. It's all about Burgers, Dogs, Sides, and Many Meaty Things ... what fun!

Want even more?

Go to Jorj.com and sign up for the I CAN COOK ANY THING app. You'll find instructional videos, links to Jorj's favorite products, more recipe substitutions, ways to use leftovers, menu suggestions, party plans, and so much more.

There's a whole community of support just waiting for you to join in!

Come along!!!!